ALSO BY BOB MITCHELL

The Heart Has Its Reasons: Reflections on Sports and Life

The Tao of Sports

How My Mother Accidentally Tossed Out My Entire Baseball-Card Collection

(and Other Sports Stories)

How My Mother Accidentally Tossed Out My Entire Baseball-Card Collection

(and Other Sports Stories)

BOB MITCHELL

FROG, LTD.
BERKELEY, CALIFORNIA

Published by
Frog, Ltd.
P.O. Box 12327
Berkeley, California 94712
Cover and book design by Nancy Koerner
Printed in the United States of America
Distributed to the book trade by Publishers Group West

Library of Congress Cataloging-in-Publication Data

Mitchell, Robert L., 1944–
     How my mother accidentally tossed out my entire baseball-card
collection : and other sports stories / Bob Mitchell
          p.   cm.
     ISBN 1-883319-88-9 (alk. paper)
     1. Sports stories, American. I. Title.
PS3563.I814H69   1999
813'.54--dc21   98-51189
                                                              CIP

1   2   3   4   5   6   7   8   9   /   03   02   01   00   99

For Diane,
the Willie Mays of friends.

Contents

Introduction

This book, written by a dedicated sports nut, is dedicated to sports nuts.

The memories, stories, essays, and ruminations that follow are the products of nearly five decades of living, loving, eating, drinking, sleeping, playing, studying, pondering, and going completely crazy ga-ga over sports.

During which time I think I've learned a few things. I've found sports to be universal, a cosmic entity with a strong appeal to an incredibly wide variety of human beings. I've also found it to be pretty profound, representing nothing less than a mirror of the human condition, a virtual reflection of the best and the worst in us.

But above all, I've found sports to be constantly *inspiring*.

Sports inspires passion, and so passion is an integral part of my stories, in the forms of joy, hatred, love, brotherhood, friendship, enthusiasm, satisfaction, admiration, awe, competition, pride, envy, anger, pleasure, ecstasy, obsession, creativity, struggle, and suffering.

Sports inspires nostalgia, and so I've summoned from deep within me many of the memories that have (lo these many decades) yearned to be free: Spaldeens in the driveway, summer camp, transistor radios, the echoes of infield chatter, baseball-card collecting, fraternity houses, rivalries, clay caked on my adolescent tennis sneakers.

Sports inspires fascination, and so I've written about sports of all shapes and colors. From the "major" ones like baseball, basketball, football, tennis, golf, soccer, and hockey to less familiar ones no less wondrous: hangerball, pennyball, wallball, scuba diving, rollerblading, poker, frog-racing, catch. Taking place in locales as varied as Boro Park and Williamstown, Columbus and West Lafayette, Maine and Texas, Maui and Tel Aviv. And with story-lines that I've found to be ceaselessly thought-provoking. The cosmic significance of baseball cards. The genetic ramifications of tossing a hardball. The quest to determine the hairiest NBA player ever. The tragic nature of rooting. The proper way to name your dog. A brief history of hats. The relationship of sports to Latin. The tiny place in the brain where all trivia is stored. The deep message behind winning and losing. The therapeutic effects of on-field regurgitation.

So, from one sports nut to another, let me offer you, in the spirit of sharing, my memories and stories and thoughts. Hoping you'll find them as inspiring to read as I've found them to live.

And I'll leave you with a sports quote, one of my all-time favorites. These immortal (and inspiring) words were uttered by Wes Westrum, former N.Y. Giants backstop, then-manager of the woeful Mets, and a man not particularly renowned for his verbal acuity. When asked what he thought about a thrilling extra-inning victory over the Cubs, he paused for a moment, scratched his head, and replied, "It was a real *cliff-dweller!*"

More than anything else I could possibly say, that just about sums it up.

How My Mother Accidentally Tossed Out My Entire Baseball-Card Collection

You did *WHAT???!!!##@!!??!* *★★!%@#!??!???????*

The fateful year was 1962. October 8, to be exact. And (give or take an exclamation point) this was my precise reaction when I learned of the Dastardly Deed from my mother's own lips. Of the devastating news that, innocently and with no apparent knowledge of wrongdoing, she had disposed of my entire baseball-card collection, tossed it right into the garbage can. Lock, stock, and proverbial barrel. *My own mother!*

Which begs the deeply disturbing metaphysical question: how could the very same person who went through the pain, torment, and discomfort of nine months of gestation plus the actual delivery of a human being commit such an egregious crime against that human being, a crime of such towering magnitude as to affect his entire life and deprive him of riches (emotional and fiduciary) beyond measure? Huh?

Just as I suspected. You *have* no answer. How *could* you? The question is transparently rhetorical and thus defies a reasonable response.

It's just like asking, "How could Medea have slain her own flesh and blood?" or "How could Branca have stuck with the fastball?"

And through time (it has been exactly thirty-five years since The Deed was committed), I have replayed again and again and again what I assume to have been the Actual Act over and over and over in my mind, in a vain attempt to make some sense of it. And my efforts have, time after time, proven—alas!—to be to no avail. Fruitless. Futile. Abortive.

Here's how my re-enactment of The Crime goes. I'm away at college, freshman year. And there's my mother at home, doing her usual twice-a-day clean-up of my (old, newly-abandoned) room. Dusting. Sweeping. And, naturally, re-arranging. And generally making the room look *presentable* (in case, of course, the President of the United States or Queen Elizabeth should just happen to be strolling through the Hasidic Boro Park section of Brooklyn, of a Thursday afternoon). I'd left a number of personal possessions at home, which I assumed were *still* my personal possessions and would remain untouched until I myself might decide to jettison them. Anyway, there's Mom re-arranging, and she suddenly spies, on a shelf in my bookcase, three or four overstuffed and impressive-looking Composition Books. You know the kind: those "log books" with the funny black-and-white speckled covers that we used for penmanship in grade school. The kind people use for *important* stuff, *official* stuff, *private* stuff. *Overstuffed with what?*, you might ask. Why, with an exceedingly large amount of baseball cards. Cards I'd been collecting painstakingly for, oh, maybe a dozen years. Cards arranged in excruciating order, alphabetically and according to teams and batting averages and ERAs. And what else is lying there on the shelf just minding its own business? Well, sir, on that same shelf there are also five or six shoeboxes, brimming to the top, about to explode from their own plenitude. And sticking out of which are baseball cards that just can't be held in check. Wildly, energetically thrusting themselves outward, as if crying to be deposited in...yet another shoebox! Yep, these invaluable and important-looking artifacts sure look exactly like—for all the world and to the naked, untrained eye—*things you'd never in your wildest dreams imagine someone could, knowingly or unknowingly, dispose of, toss out, or otherwise contemplate trashing.*

So there's my Mom innocently dusting and re-arranging one Thursday afternoon. So she spies all these *important-looking* artifacts and, well, let's see. Inspecting them for a fleeting second, she whispers to herself, "Hmmmm, these *could* be important artifacts and maybe they mean something to my dear, wonderful son. And after all, they *are* in his room and they *are* still his very own private possessions, even though he's flown from the nest. And boy-oh-boy, it sure looks like he's invested a whole lot of time lovingly arranging, collecting, and hoarding them. And he *is* a sports nut, so they're probably still *very* dear to his heart. And, you know, it would probably be inappropriate to throw them all out without at least consulting him, without asking him personally whether he'd like to keep them or to have me throw them in the garbage. And I've even seen him spend hours and hours with them, when he was a kid, so I'm guessing they probably still mean a great deal to him, physically, emotionally, and spiritually. And look! Look at all these little 3½" × 2½" cardboard cards that used to give him so much pleasure! Cards that he spent many of the joyful hours of his youth arranging in these log books and keeping in these shoeboxes! Cards that he used to take out on special occasions (like when the sun came up in the morning) to flip endlessly on the carpeted floor of his bedroom (*heads or tails*) or against his bedroom wall (*leaners*)! And look! [She flips through the cards in one of the shoeboxes.] Look at all his favorite cards and players! Why, there's Coot Veal and Cot Deal and Turk Lown and old, wizened Alpha Brazle and Sibby Sisti and Sam Jethroe and Herm Wehmeier and Bud Podbielan and Don Mossi and Roy Smalley and Johnny

Klippstein and Billy Loes and Duane Pillette and Luke Easter and Roy Sievers and Matt Batts and Phil Cavarretta and Chris Van Cuyk and Johnny Wyrostek and Dave Jolly and Virgil Jester (I *know* he got a kick out of the fact that these two were on the same team) and Stan Palys and Peanuts Lowrey and Solly Hemus and all his beloved Giants (even Tookie Gilbert and Sal Yvars and Max Lanier and Alex Konikowski) and Wayne Terwilliger and Eddie Yost the Walking Man and Minnie Minoso and Ned Garver and Erv Palica and Sid Hudson and Ike Delock and Ferris Fain and Gus Zernial and Al Zarilla and Granny Hamner and bespectacled Earl Torgeson and Carlos Paula and Reno Bertoia and Saul Rogovin and Dee Fondy and Clint Courtney and Vinegar Bend Mizell! [Now she puts her right index finger, ever-so-thoughtfully, against her closed lips.] And . . . *naaaaaaaaaaaaaah*, he probably doesn't want them anymore, and besides, they look like junk!" And so, without a second thought, without a glimmer of hesitation, she gathers them all up in her arms, all three or four overstuffed Composition Books and all five or six impressive-looking shoeboxes, and lugs them to the garbage can outside in the alley. And there, with no earthly witnesses to gaze upon this Unspeakable Act, she tosses them into the can and, with a sweet smile, returns to complete her various Duties of Cleanliness and Godliness.

Well, there it is. Every time I replay The Act in my mind, the exact chronology, specific description, and precise movements are always the same, never changing a whit, just as I have painfully described them. And for many years (when I was younger and more cynical), I would hold The Deed against my mother (*can you imagine?*) and bring it up occasionally (*how insensitive!*) and make her feel guilty (*a pox on me!*). Yep, in my more immature days, I was under the impression that were I still in possession of my entire baseball-card collection, I could get a bundle for it if I put it up for sale. Yes, sir, *a pret-ty penny!* And maybe I could retire early and buy my own remote Mediterranean island and spend the rest of my days leisurely reading Proust and painting and playing the ocarina and swinging on my hammock. . . .

But those days are long gone, and I am over my anger and grief at the loss of my priceless cardboard buddies. All that's left is the haunting, repeated imaginary reconstruction of how my mother could ever have committed The Deed. And, in my deepest moments of self-examination, I occasionally muse about one other thing. You see, over the years, I've met a very great number of men of my generation who, like me, happen to be life-long sports nuts. And who, like me, happen to have had (for their own private pleasure and aeons before "fantasy baseball" was ever conceived) immense, invaluable baseball-card collections kept in log books and shoeboxes and arranged in excruciating order, alphabetically and according to teams and batting averages and ERAs. And who, like me, had mothers who, innocently and inexplicably, tossed out their entire card collections, right there into the garbage cans. Lock, stock, and proverbial barrel. And I wonder to myself whether all these Terrible Deeds were in fact just coincidental: isolated acts that just happened to occur *all the time*, decade after decade. Or maybe, just maybe, they occurred far too frequently and in too many geographic and demographic areas and over too long a time and to too many unsuspecting young men just going off to college to be, well, unrelated.

And the more I wonder, the more convinced I am that there are actually *three* phenomena that you can absolutely count on: death, taxes, and your mother accidentally tossing out your entire baseball-card collection.

Missing Chromosome

I was having a catch the other day with my best friend, Diane.

It was just another catch: two people, two mitts, a hardball. Back and forth, back and forth. You throw it to me, I throw it to you. Pretty routine stuff for most people, I guess. What made it feel even more routine was the fact that it's the same catch I'd been having with great regularity for probably forty-six years or so. With my father first. Then my friends. Then my children. Always the same. Back and forth, back and forth.

We were having a great time giggling, bantering, and, well, catching, when I had an unannounced epiphany: *I suddenly realized the terrible beauty of this ritual!* And I saw that, in a funny way, the very act was sufficient to justify life on this planet as we know it.

Now I admit that's quite a statement, and for an instant, I myself was skeptical of its breadth and ambition. But, if you accept for a moment that life in its most wondrous state is nothing more or less than the joy of the moment, that what is past and what is future don't really exist, and that this existential instant is all we have, then (if you've ever had a catch yourself) you'll agree that what we're talking about is a feeling that is fundamentally and unexpurgatedly joyous and, peculiarly, like no other. A feeling that allows us to focus totally inside a cocoon of delight and, as Thoreau might have put it, to cease to exist and begin to be.

I was becoming aware of the magnificence of this thought; and, in an effort to share it with my companion, I made an attempt to express the inner joy and radiance one feels as one goes through the repetitive and seemingly jejune motions of the act itself. The moment was peculiarly intense; I had never before felt compelled to share these intimate feelings with another human being, male *or* female.

First, I begin, there's the wonderful (and required) preparation for the reception of the pellet. The pounding of the glove, the folding of the glove, the hugging of the knees, the rocking back and forth, the internal chatter, to say nothing of the *emotional* experience of anticipation. (For pop-ups, I add parenthetically, there's also the "getting a bead" on the ball, requiring acute judgment, spatial feel, a sense of contextualizing oneself with the sun, the clouds, the sky, and, by extension, the cosmos itself.)

Then, I continue, there is footwork to consider. The terpsichorean patter, as feet gauge distance, height, and depth, making excruciating split decisions at the same time side to side, forward and back.

And, as ball finally enters glove, there's the ineffable joy to be savored of the pop of the mitt, the sensuous union of cowhide on cowhide, a sound so sweet it almost makes you want to moo with pleasure.

But, I go on, that's the mere tip of the proverbial iceberg. (At this crucial point, Diane tries unsuccessfully to muffle a slightly patronizing guffaw.) Now, I insist, comes the throwing part, the *yang* of the catch, the complementary firing after the loading, the giving after the receiving, the resolution of the eternally-renewing quid pro quo.

Y'see, first ya gotta think about The Motion and *whose* you're gonna use. (Another vaguely muffled guffaw.) Do we choose the infielder's, complete with feisty, Stankyesque grimace, deftness, and controlled fury in an effort to nip the jackrabbit runner speeding to first? (Ashburn? Bruton? Covington? Boyd?) Or do we go with a pitcher's windup and delivery, but, again, *whose*? Maglie's sneering, no-nonsense, brushback, don't-screw-with-me offering? A cute lefty's tantalizing, peek-a-boo approach? (Haddix? Shantz?) Marichal's, complete with exaggerated kick? Or perhaps a no-windup deal, reminiscent of the only World Series perfecto? (The guffaw is now not quite so polite and muffled but—accompanied by a vacuous, almost pitiful stare—is actually gaining a supercilious and slightly impatient momentum.)

Then there's the tapping of ball on glove. This is *real* important. Superfluous, mannered, overly idiosyncratic, maybe, but the *sine qua non* of the throw. Necessary accompaniment of the cockiness and strength that feeds into the motion itself.

And once the projectile is released, I persist, there is the all-important follow-through. Which, if practiced properly, freezes us in an immortal pose (for a fleeting second, yes, but one replete with rhapsodic ecstasy), a pose that imaginary cameras capture for our own personal Topps baseball card, or perhaps it is a journalist's, catching us in our last, triumphant toss as we clinch Game 7, a moment to be developed, submitted, and printed in the Sunday *Times* Section 5. (The guffaws now explode into a steady, mocking stream of ribald laughter.)

This entire process has a beauty of its own, to be sure. But, I rant on, it is the repetition of the act, each time in the form of a nuanced variation (different pitcher, different infielder, different motion: sidearm, overhand, three-quarters), that creates a ceaselessly nuanced panoply of kaleidoscopic possibilities. A Zen-like rhythm creating a focus that is uninterruptible (except, when we were younger, by our mother's cry of *"dinner's ready!"*), each toss and reception embodying a trance-like mantra that must be obeyed by a spirituality residing deep within.

.   Diane has collapsed on the ground in a fetal position, laughing hysterically, uncontrollably. Her mitt lies by her side, and the two eerily resemble victim and weapon at a murder scene. By now, I realize that, despite my liberal free-thinking attitudes about equality and equal rights, there is truly a huge, fundamental, and demarcating chasm between man and woman. Something that goes way beyond the presence or absence of audible flatus and eructation. I realize, suddenly and definitively, that besides (and even more than) genitalia, the comparative enjoyment, appreciation, and love of the high seriousness of The Act of Having a Catch is what truly differentiates the sexes. It is a palpable, nearly physical characteristic that is somehow embedded in the genetic material of the American male and (with very few exceptions) not in that of the female.

All of which allows me to conclude this tale with my new theory of The Creation story: maybe Adam and Eve weren't really tossed out of Eden after all! My guess is that they were probably having a catch (with an apple, of course: baseballs weren't created until much later); Eve must've tired of Adam's self-absorbed lecturing on the ecstasy of The Act (he had, after all, just eaten from the Tree of Knowledge); and the latter undoubtedly left in a huff, in search of a *guy* with whom to share the ineffable joys of pegging and snaring, sempiternally, the vermilion spheroid.

Hirsutest

To answer Al Michaels' rhetorical question of 1980: *yes!* And one of the many miracles of sports that I believe in is that in an instant, it can make close friends out of total strangers.

I was writing TV commercials at a large New York ad agency in the winter of 1991 when I get a call from a music guy named Fred Thaler. One of thousands of typical calls writers get from reps, composers, photographers, directors, producers, voice-over people, talent agents, and similar "suppliers" to sell their wares. You don't have the time to see many of these people, as nice and talented as they may be, because, well, time is money. And in the wonderful world of advertising, free time is about as rare as Manny Sanguillen taking on the first pitch.

For some reason, though, I decide to see Fred one dank December morning. I knew him, by reputation, to be a nice guy and a very talented musician and song writer. I knew his wife also, and things were unusually slow at the office that week, so what the hell.

And what I anticipate to be just another polite, routine meeting with some music guy turns out to be a wonderful morning to remember and, as Claude Rains would have said, "the beginning of a beautiful friendship."

Soon after we exchange the appropriate niceties and engage in a brief conversation regarding commercials, music, composition, arranging, and assorted requisite issues that could possibly persuade us of the wisdom of a potential collaboration, we somehow stumble upon the subject of sports.

Within seconds, it becomes obvious that we share a passion, a lunacy, an obsession for anything having to do with the topic. We first alternate stories (as children masquerading as grown men are wont to do) of bygone days. His playing college roundball, my soccer and tennis exploits. His rubbing elbows with Alcindor, my baseball caught off the bat of Davey Williams during an exhibition game (Jints and Bosox) in June of '54.

As we segue into the inexhaustible realm of trivia, I notice that our relationship is also turning the corner: we are no longer supplier and client, but nascent friends with that special bond sports nuts can only share with others of their peculiar ilk. Our demeanors change abruptly from a calculated professional civility to a passionate and focused fanaticism, with all the classic symptoms: wide eyes, warm glows, silly grins, boundless enthusiasm.

We spend a huge chunk of time discussing a number of burning queries that constantly preoccupy us both and about which we're both passionate. Which batter had the widest stance in MLB history? (*Ironically, a pitcher on the '54 Giants, Alex Konikowski.*) Which player made Knicks fans most nervous when he put the ball on the floor? (*A flat-footed tie between Ron Sobie and Phil Jackson.*) Which major-college varsity hoopster was the best tennis player? (*It was, of course, Northwestern's Marty Riessen.*) Which announcer does the best color commentary? (*Another tie: Tim McCarver, Mary Carillo, Ken Venturi.*) Which athlete/team fash-

ioned the greatest upset ever? (*Yet another tie: Jack Fleck, Texas Western.*)
Who was the best college running back of Italian descent? (*Bellino nips
Cappelletti.*)

The hours whiz by (by now, we're well into our fourth, and time—
usually an enemy of Marvellian, even Baudelairean proportions—has
miraculously become an old buddy). After meandering through most of
the major categories of trivia and useless factoids, at one point we
become entangled in what can best be described as a fight-to-the-finish,
dog-eat-dog, febrile exchange concerning a question that is probably
uppermost in every true sports fan's mind: *Who was the hairiest NBA
player of all time?*

Sounds pretty silly, I admit, but as true sports fanatics, we pursue the
issue with the intensity of a Lincoln-Douglas debate (or, if you prefer, a
Botvinnik-Smyslov chess match). Back and forth we go, constantly
amending our previous assertions as our frenzied minds search for yet
another hoopster to supersede the prior one. As one of us racks his brain
and visual memory for yet another simian body to proffer, the other
always seems to shout a new offering at the top of his lungs, almost as if
to goad the dialogue into another level of frenzy.

"Vinnie Boryla!" I shout gleefully, hoping for the checkmate.

"Not bad," Fred admits, "but how 'bout *Vern Mikkelson*, huh?"

"You mother!" I retort calmly. "But," I continue, as if swooping in
on his unprotected king, "what about *Pettit*?"

Five-second pause. Then, Fred blurts out his definitive, unswayable
final offering. Enunciating with delicious precision, he lances the deadly
dart: **"NEAL WALK!!!"**

For a brief second, I panic, fearing the worst. Does he HAVE me?
Do I admit the terrible truth, concede, and go home with my tail
between my legs? NO! I am a fighter, not a quitter. Every instinct, every
fiber of my competitive athletic being rebels against the prospect of
throwing in the towel. I grit my teeth, screw up my eyes, furl my brow,
and go into a momentary trance. My visual memory clicks into reverse,

like some crazed Ann Arbor microfilm whirring backwards, searching for some answer, *any* answer! Let's see . . . nineties . . . eighties . . . seventies . . . sixties . . . fifties . . . fifties . . . AH-*HAH!!!!!!!!!*

Looking deep into my new-found friend's eyes, and with the self-assurance of someone confirming a winning Bingo card, I announce my undebatable, irrefutable solution.

"CHAR-LIE TY-RA!!!!!!!!!!"

After arguing our cases back and forth for a time, we laugh, shake hands, and call it a stalemate. After all, it's getting late, and we each have to return to our respective realities. We part, with the wonderful, warm feeling of having met a soulmate, of having made a friend.

So, sounds like the story's over? Not even *close*! Because, as any true sports fanatic would do, I *had* to resolve the issue, to find out *once and for all* who was hairier!

I end up spending that entire afternoon on the phone doing the most intense research I'd done since grad school. First, I call the offices of The University of Louisville, The University of Florida, the New York Knicks, and the Phoenix Suns in search of 8" × 10" glossies. No luck. One of the offices, however, tips me onto a sports collector in Portland who might have some snapshots of Walk. No luck. Then I call the headquarters of the NBA, which shunts me off to three or four different functionaries in various sections of its corporate catacombs, until I'm finally able to convince someone of my integrity and the gravity of my situation. Grudgingly, he agrees to send whatever he has. My job is completed by dusk, and I return home with the knowledge that I'd done my utmost as a hoop sleuth. Now all I have to do is wait for the mail to confirm my wisdom and Fred's abysmal ignorance!

The days pass, and I've forgotten all about it after a week or so (by then, things at the office had picked up considerably). Until one bright Saturday morning, a brown package arrives from the NBA.

"All RIGHT!" I chortle, smelling the sweet aroma of victory wafting from within the well-protected missive. Opening it with the care and delicacy of an Arctic fox eviscerating a newly-caught hare, I empty the contents and let them cascade gently onto the surface of my desk. But after viewing the enclosed pictures, I immediately lapse into a temporary coma. Because staring back at me are, first, a glossy head-and-shoulder of Neal Walk, as damning a piece of evidence as has ever been laid before a jury. Neal—generally, a good-looking guy—is pictured there, smiling in his spanking clean Knicks jersey, his chest and shoulders covered wall-to-wall with a thick layer of what appears to be Lon Chaney's werewolf costume. To make matters worse, his lycanthropic face (with the sole exception of his boyish cheeks) is thick, redolent even, with bushy hair, and his head hair flows in a steady line into his thick, full, Rutherford B. Hayes-like beard.

Clearly, I am dead meat. Road pizza. Coyote vittles.

But I have one chance for a reprieve: Charlie Tyra's glossy could surpass even Neal's, proving me the victor, the superior, the more knowledgeable. BUT NO!!! HORRORS!!! As my eyes pan to Charlie's glossy, the awful truth reveals itself right there, a black-and-white prima-facie piece of evidence, if ever there was one. There's Tyra posing (pictured as a Louisville frosh), with face, chest, and shoulders as clean and bare as a baby's *tuchis*. Not a single hair to be found anywhere! I take out my art director's loupe and scour his body for some hair, a follicle, *anything!!!*

Zilch.

I can scarcely believe my eyes.

A few days later, Fred and I have a good laugh about my research and subsequent disappointment. And being a gentleman, he grants me—by executive etiquette—a tie, seeing as how Charlie was probably just as hirsute as Neal, that the photo was probably taken just before his follicular sprouting had proliferated, and that it was probably doctored, airbrushed, and otherwise retouched by the Louisville AD for purposes of publicity.

I guess what's important about all this is that we had become—and still are—steadfast friends, bonded together by the glue of a profound love of things sporting. And, moreover, that sports fanatics will spare no effort in their tireless search for the answers to the stupidest rhetorical questions imaginable.

But, Charlie, if you ever read this and happen to have a graphic picture of yourself taken in the late '50s that reveals your true manliness, please contact my agent and send it on to my home address. I'd *really* appreciate it. Because it would help confirm the feeling that I've always had, deep down, where it really counts: when it comes to naming the hairiest player in NBA history, there is *no one* who can surpass my skill and erudition.

Famous
Jewish Hockey
Players

How Do I Hate Thee?

Let me count the ways:
1. You stink.
2. You smell.
3. You make me miserable.
4. You befoul my life.
5. You sully my existence.
6. You make me sick to my stomach.
7. You make me wanna puke.
8. You give me hives.
9. You are a wart on the face of the human species.
10. You are a blot on the escutcheon of *homo sapiens*.

Such were my feelings—and probably those of every other self-respecting New York fan of the mid-to-late-fifties—every time Dolph Schayes drove the lane against our pathetic, beloved Knicks. Such was the passion, the unabated and pure hatred that we collectively felt, that we spewed forth continuously against this most annoying of all Nats.

How strange it is—and how wonderful!—that, as humans, we can FEEL our feelings (albeit of utter negativity), we can vent them, express them, give audible form to them! How noble that we ordinary fans, we average rooters of the overpaid, we mere underlings are capable of reaching heights of passion that so few others can reach or have ever reached! Who else but the fan (and especially the New York fan), what other dark and tragic figure can better express, with such fervor and eloquence, the vitriol and disgust he feels for his fate? Oedipus? Don't make me laugh! O.K., let's compare:

OEDIPUS: Lost! Ah lost! At last it's blazing clear.
              Light of my days, go dark. I want to gaze no more.
KNICKS FAN: Get that bastard! Knock him down! Smash
              his face, kick his teeth in! Squish his butt!
              STOP THAT SON-OF-A-BITCH!!!

King Lear? A mere amateur in the relative exuding of bile:

LEAR: Blow, winds, and crack your cheeks! Rage! Blow!
KNICKS FAN: HEY! Stop that hairy freak! Give him a forearm
              to the kishkes! Send him to the goddam hospital!

To be fair, actually, one of the many lessons that sports teaches us is that underlying all our passion is a basic respect we fans have for the object of this hatred. I think that all the athletes I've "hated" throughout my career as a fan are precisely those I would've *killed* for to get on my team. And of all of them, there are four who jump right to the top of the list.

In basketball, it was Schayes. Dolph was a wonderfully gifted player for the Syracuse Nationals (and, at the end, for Philly). He enjoyed a sixteen-year Hall of Fame career, from 1948–64, and averaged over 18 ppg over that span. But much more than that, he was a tough, rugged, aggressive, in-your-face player who just would not be denied when he drove the lane. He was a master at protecting the ball and at getting fouled for a three-point play (in the days before three-point plays). On top of all that, he had a magnificent set shot from way out (in the days when you took set shots). Worst of all, he would, almost like clockwork, beat my Knicks in tight games at the last second with one of his patented inside moves. There I'd be, in bed on a school night, listening to my black Emerson transistor under my pillow so my parents wouldn't catch me. Marty Glickman would be doing the play-by-play. And with three seconds to go—it was always three for some arcane reason, never two or four—ol' Dolph would inexorably drive the lane, sink a layup, get fouled by Gallatin or Clifton, and win the game with no time left. "CRAP!" I'd yell out, risking a parental visit. Seems like it happened virtually every night, same scenario, same Schayes driving for the winning layup.

God, did I hate him!

In baseball, it was Jackie Robinson. I was a die-hard Giants fan growing up in Brooklyn (talk about tragic figures!), and Jackie was one of the most incredible (thus, infuriating) players I've ever seen. I mean, there was no one else like him, before or since. He just had a *sense* of what to do on the field. He was a gifted natural athlete (also a track, football, and basketball star at UCLA before he got to the majors), but on top of all that, he had an instinct that was absolutely uncanny. In fact, you'd have trouble finding a better natural all-around athlete in the history of modern sports than ol' number 42.

He would *kill* my beloved Jints, with his fielding, his hitting, his bunting, his power, his clutch hits, but especially with his base-running. He was crafty, smart, and tricky, using his speed, his elusiveness, and his instinct to make exactly the right play, whatever the situation was.

Once he was on first base as Russ Meyer (I think) was pitching a no-hitter against Dem Bums. A grounder was hit in the hole between first and second, and without hesitation, Jackie reached down and caught it. HE CAUGHT IT!!!!!!! He knew, of course, that in so doing, he would be called out automatically. But he also knew that the batter would be awarded a hit and that Meyer's confidence would be destroyed because his no-hitter would now be a one-hitter. And sure enough it was. And sure enough, the Dodgers eventually won the game. Talk about brilliance and pure instinct.

On another occasion, the count was oh-and-two, and the pitcher uncorked a wild pitch, I mean a *really* wild pitch. Without hesitating, Jackie took a wild swing, striking himself out. He knew, of course, that the catcher would never retrieve the ball in time to throw him out, so he swung and sauntered down to first base unmolested. And these were only a few of the endless examples of how Jackie could beat you. And he usually did when the Dodgers were playing the Giants.

God, did I hate him!

(P.S. I'll never forget the day he was traded to the Giants—for Dick Littlefield!—at the very end of his career. December 13, 1956. I was walking home from Hessing's, the corner luncheonette in my Boro Park childhood Brooklyn neighborhood, when I saw the back-page headlines in the *New York Post*. I must admit, I was ecstatic: we were finally gonna get Jackie on *our* side, and he'd help us beat the Dodgers every time!!! Of course, the next day, because he was fierce-ly loyal and probably saw the writing on the wall, he refused to be traded and retired immediately. I've never been so happy and so sad in a twenty-four hour period, before or since!)

In football, the guy I hated most was Roger Staubach. The Detestable Dodger. (Maybe that added to my hatred, the fact that his nickname was "Dodger," given my loyalty to the baseball Giants.) Again, the reason I hated him so much was that he used to *kill* my football Giants, to whom I'd been loyal since '51. Roger was, for me, the greatest running quarterback ever. He was as strong as Randall Cunningham, and maybe just as tricky as Tark, who could be pretty tricky. But Roger was so incredibly elusive. He always seemed barely to escape the grasp of would-be tacklers. I mean *barely*. When he played the Giants, I always knew him as The Mother, not The Dodger, because I would always scream *Get The Mother!* to the defense every single time he ran the ball. But with rare exceptions, they never would.

God, did I hate him!

And in hockey, it was a little guy named Johnny McKenzie. Johnny was the least dazzling of a wonderful Boston Bruins line during the sixties that also featured Fred Stanfield and Johnny Bucyk. Mac didn't score as much as the other two, but when the hated Bruins played my Broadway Blues, he'd really piss me off. The guy was a proverbial waterbug, scooting around, getting under the Rangers' skins. You'd knock him down and he'd pop back up. He was incredible in the corners: he'd always be there, fighting and scraping and scrapping and clawing for the puck. He was really short—seems like he was 5'6" or something—but he'd always get into fights with guys eight inches taller and 100 pounds heavier. And he always seemed to hold his own, the scrappy little bastard.

God, did I hate him!

So that's my Pantheon of Hate. Schayes. Robinson. Staubach. McKenzie. Four of the greatest professional competitors I've ever seen. Four of the athletes whom, retrospectively, I've most respected. And most important, the four guys who have allowed me, as a fan, to reach the pinnacle of catharsis, of venting my Pity and my Fear, as Aristotle would have put it.

God, did I hate them!!!!!!!!!!!!!!!!!!!!!!!!!!!!!!!!!!!

I Think I Just Died and Went to Heaven

To create the heavens and the earth and the firmament and the seasons and the fish of the sea and the birds of the air and all the other living creatures plus man and woman, it took God six days. Coincidentally, that's precisely how long I spent in the kingdom beyond the pearly gates. Or, to use its more formal nomenclature, *The Six-Day Tennis Fantasy Camp with John Newcombe and the Legends*.

A once-in-a-lifetime, pinch-me-to-make-sure-I'm-not-dreaming, I-can't-believe-it's-really-happening-to-me six-pack of days tailored to satisfy every craving of the most hopelessly insatiable tennis fanatic that all took place in New Braunfels, Texas, October 20–25, 1996.

I first get wind of it through my good friend and tennis buddy, Joel Drucker, a first-rate journalist and tennis writer (and also a helluva player), at the Berkeley Tennis Club. Six days of grueling, intensely competitive tennis at Newk's splendid tennis ranch located thirty miles NE of San Antonio, raves Druck. Spent with the likes of Newk and Rosewall and Emerson and Stolle and Roche and Davidson and

Anderson and Pasarell and Riessen and Drysdale. All rallying with, coaching, ballboying for, ribbing, ridiculing, encouraging, instructing, and staying-up-till-the-wee-hours-drinking-Foster's-and-discussing-the-good-ol'-days with sixty-four "campers" who'd enroll from all over the U.S. and beyond.

(*Right.* And I'll also be signing up real soon for a weekend of jamming, fungo, and witty repartee with Eric Clapton, Willie Mays, and Neil Simon!)

Of course, it all sounds way too good to be true, and besides, it's humongously expensive. (To give you an idea, the pricetag is exactly the same as that of a Cadillac my father bought in 1960!) Naturally, I cast the idea out of my mind, at least for a few weeks. But somehow it keeps returning, beckoning to me like a Siren to one of Odysseus' men. Ah, to be coached by Newk! To shoot the bull with Davo and Emmo! To rally with Charlie and Mal and Rochie! To discuss nuances with Muscles and Marty! To banter and cajole with Cliffie and Fiery Fred! Those dichotomous "devil" and "angel" cartoon characters constantly pop up in thought balloons above my head with their carping dialogue:

"Hey, you'll *never* get this chance again, y'know?"

"Maybe, but what corporation's gonna subsidize you?"

"C'mon, you wuss, don't blow it!"

"Yeah? An' jus' who's gonna foot the bill?"

"You're gonna die a lonely man, with no beautiful tennis memories!"

"You're gonna die a pauper, having spent your last penny on this cockamamey escapade!"

I desperately need a tie-breaker. And—lo and behold!—at that very moment comes my miracle: the advance for the two books I'm writing at the time just happens to arrive from my publisher. Without hesitating an instant, I pounce upon the fiduciary opportunity, call Steve Contardi (the Cincinnati pro who's the organizing force behind the camp), send in my check, and am officially enrolled! But

that's the easy part: now I must prepare body and mind for this ultimate challenge.

For starters, I had just gone through the ineffably excruciating
experience of attempting to pass a kidney stone. On top of that, I
know all too well that my chronic, scoliotic, inherited bad back won't
allow me to play on consecutive days, much less six straight days, five
or six hours per, of grueling competitive tennis. So, against my will (I
am, after all, the son of a pathologist, whose medical persona is the
mongoose to the chiropractor's cobra), I consult a local chiropractor,
who bequeaths to me a thirty-minute routine of back-stretching and
abdominal-strengthening exercises, which I do without fail, twice a
day, for the next four months.

Simultaneously, I contact Mark Garrison, the head tennis pro at
the local Sonoma Mission Inn. He agrees on a program of hitting
with me: an hour and a half, two to three times a week, which we do
religiously for four months. Besides being a great guy, Mark has the
perfect game for me to work on mine: lots of pace and wonderful
control. We play intense, hard-fought matches; after a few weeks, my
game is approaching the level it had reached in the late fifties and
early sixties, when I was playing junior tournaments as a teen-ager
and, later, on the Williams College freshman team. My groundies
regain their steadiness of old, eschewing unforced errors as in days of
yore; my serve, known for its control and spin but surely never for its
power, suddenly develops unaccustomed velocity and pace; and
strokes that had lain fallow for decades (nay, scores!)—the exquisitely
disguised dropshot, the nastily-angled crosscourt forehand, the
wicked topspin lob, the nefarious backhand-pass-down-the-line, the
feared lunging stop-volley—experience a sudden renaissance. After a
few months of hitting sessions, my game is as solid and dependable as
it has ever been, as it is probably ever going to get. Because I manage
somehow to win a few matches and to stay in most of them, my confidence is high. And mentally, I'm prepared for the most grueling,

exhausting five-hour, five-set match that any opponent could ever put me through.

Between Mark's good-natured coaching, the wonderfully salubrious effects of our matches, and the hundreds of monastic hours spent on the floor of my study doing my back exercises, I leave for Newk's tennis ranch as well prepared as any toughened warrior going off to do battle with the most indomitable of foes.

The days preceding my departure are likewise filled with rigorous mental preparation. Druck warns me that Newk and he have an ongoing competition based on tennis trivia and welcomes my joining forces with him to posit an unbeatable Yankee phalanx against the menacing Aussie aggressor. I am already well armed, having been present at virtually every U.S. Open (pre-'68: Nationals) since 1951 and having spent a large portion of my fifty-two years gorging my cerebral crevices with every possible sort of sports trivia, many of which happen to be of the tennis variety. But to sharpen these weapons, I fortify myself with a daily diet of reading—mostly of Bud Collins' *Modern Encyclopedia of Tennis*—which hones the spear that is my tennis erudition. Now I am even further armed with the addition of dazzlingly voluminous (and utterly useless) information concerning the likes of Herbie Flam and Budge Patty, Christophe Roger-Vasselin and Werner Fisher, "Linky" Boshoff and Linda Ferrando, Matt Anger and Hugo Chapacu.

Before I actually arrive at Newk's camp, an unexpected event happens that bears recounting. My friend Diane and I plan to spend a few days together in San Antonio prior to the camp, just for fun. Neither of us has ever visited this fair city, so we look forward to a few romantic days of strolling along the Riverwalk, moonlit Mexican dinners of authentic fajitas and gigantic margaritas, and maybe a quick peek at the Alamo. The second morning we're there, I awake at 6 A.M. in our hotel room to do my daily matutinal exercise regimen. I don my underwear, which (being a guy) I'd thrown on the floor the previous night, and commence my knee stretches. Something is amiss, I sense, as I feel a piercing pinch, (mercifully) just north of my pubic area. I jump four feet in the air, let out an unearthly yowl, and flick some wiggling object out of my shorts.

It's a scorpion!

What follows is a steady stream of well-chosen, nearly-unprintable imprecations. Something to the effect that goddamit, after all I went through, goddamit, to prepare for this once-in-a-lifetime experience—including all the goddam hitting sessions, months of goddam back exercises, a friggin' kidney stone, and an assiduous and daily attempt to avoid numerous klutzy mishaps like toe-stubbing and pulled muscles—I step one goddam foot in the goddam state of Texas and, goddamit, I not only see my first goddam scorpion, but it damn near emasculates me!

After the EMS team and the hotel manager ascend to our room, it is adjudged that no, I am not allergic to the beast's sting and no, I won't die on the eve of my transcendent adventure and no, the scorpion (which Diane had caught fearlessly and deposited in a plastic cup)—although frighteningly prehistoric- and disgusting-looking—is not a dangerously poisonous species and cannot have given me a fatal nip.

Phew!

The swelling subsides, the day races by, and morning finally arrives, this morning of Epiphany! Actually, outside it looks more like Apocalypse than Epiphany: black clouds, pelting rain, high winds.

Ah, Texas!

Being a Jew from New York, I naturally expect the worst: for the first time in its nine-year history, the fantasy camp will be completely washed out. I'm *sure* of it. The courts, under ten feet of water, will be cordoned off, everyone will be depressed, and we'll all be sent home on the second day, refund checks in our pockets, with no stories, no memories, nothing to boast about to our grandchildren. Being an Episcopalian from California, Diane reminds me that the world is essentially good, there's a reason for everything, things will get better, and maybe I should mellow out and behave with a bit more maturity and decorum.

An hour later, I drop her at her gate and am picked up at the airport by one of the ranch pros, along with two other campers. One of them is Bob O'Neill, an OB-GYN from Rhode Island. We chat happily all the way to the ranch about everything from beer to bypass surgery, dogs to Descartes, my books, his deliveries. It is an auspicious beginning, as a new friendship replaces depressing thoughts of maelstroms and rained-out dreams.

At last, we reach Newk's ranch. I collect my sack of "goodies" (complimentary tennis bag, "fantasy" T-shirts, warm-up suit, hat, etc.), unpack, put on my tennies, and head to the dining room for a spot of lunch. Around the buffet table are a few of the early-arriving campers and Newk.

NEWK!!!!!#@*****!!!**???!!!

"G'dye," he says to me casually. This icon, proud winner of five U.S., nine Wimbledon, seven Australian, and three French titles, is saying "G'dye" to *me*?

It doesn't take me very long to realize that I'm not at a tennis ranch at all, but a place that's nothing short of The Promised Land. In fact, as the initial minutes and hours pass by, I envision an imaginary sign hanging on the gazebo, which is the hub of all activity at the ranch. The sign says: *WELCOME TO HEAVEN! The rules are simple: 1. You shall not experience any feelings of shame, defeat, envy, or frustration. 2. Your days shall be filled with nothing but peace, harmony, joy, and brotherhood. 3. Each person present here shall treat all others as absolute equals, whether they be Wimbledon champs or garden-variety schlubs. 4. Whatever happens in your matches, everyone is a winner. 5. On top of all this, the food is great!*

And best of all, this is no figment of my imagination: it's all true. Seriously! As I meet the inhabitants of this Fantasyland and begin to

soak in its atmosphere, I snicker scornfully at Santayana's solemn pro-
nouncement: *Ideal society is a drama enacted in the imagination.* Hey
George, I ain't makin' this place up!

So exactly what makes it heaven?

It all starts with the simple recipe dreamed up by Steve Contardi,
the Cincinnati pro who'd been to a baseball fantasy camp and
thought it'd work for tennis. (Boy, does it!) First, throw together
sixty-four guys who are mostly very good players and all absolute
tennis nuts, and you've got a pretty good start. Then, fold them into
an impressive tennis ranch with impeccable courts, facilities, and lay-
out, along with an outstanding group of ranch professionals and a
splendid support staff. Add ten of the absolute greatest pros in the
history of the planet (mostly Aussies), with a combined 101 Grand
Slam titles. Then mix them all up in a program of total immersion—
six days of tennis, basically from 8 A.M. till 6 P.M., including intensely
competitive matches, drills with the pros, clinics on the basics and the
nuances, "hitalongs," exhibitions, "fantasy matches," and rap sessions—
and create an atmosphere of the purest kind of male bonding, total
support, fun, kibitzing, drinking beer, and sitting around schmoozing
about every imaginable aspect of the game, and there you have it:
proverbial pigs in shit! Oh: and add, just for good measure, Larry
Starr, one of the world's greatest athletic trainers (in case of the
inevitable mishaps, tears, strains, aches, and pains); and Russ Adams,
one of the world's greatest athletic photographers (to take everyone's
pictures—in action, at the bar, with teammates, with the pros—which
we'll all bring home as keepsakes and undoubtedly use as fabulistic
fodder for our grandchildren).

The sixty-four campers (this year, forty-three are returnees, some
for the eighth and ninth times; I am a lowly rookie) share the common bond of a deep love for the game, as fans and players. Yet they're
a diverse group, representing a wide gamut of professions and geographic areas. Many are (obviously successful) business entrepreneurs,

but there are a couple of writers, a few tennis pros, some teachers and stockbrokers, a solicitor and a smattering of attorneys, a radiologist, a pulmonologist, a cardiologist, an OB-GYN, even a sheep rancher and an inventor! They hail from Australia, the U.K., Germany, and fourteen states, from Maine to New Mexico.

The bonding and camaraderie go on unabashedly and uninterruptedly each day, from the first bite of breakfast to the last Foster's at the bar at 2 A.M. The dialogue we share is mostly about tennis, but it frequently dips into related areas like epistemology and oenology, philosophy and theosophy, population and copulation. (Plus joke-telling is extremely popular!) By the end of the week, I make many good acquaintances and a handful of good friends. In the latter group, I include Druck—true eclectic, fierce competitor, stealthy southpaw, master schmoozer—whose friendship remains ever steadfast to this day; Marc Segan, inventor, Princeton grad, caustic wit, soulmate, and aficionado (as am I) of the palindrome (he bequeaths to me two new excellent exemplars: "A slut nixes sex in Tulsa" and "Go hang a salami; I'm a lasagna hog!"); Mark Cripps, an ebullient Brit from Wimbledon who, back home, teaches tennis to wayward youths and with whom I am constantly engaged in ribald (and raucous) repartee regarding issues as disparate as hairshirts and heterosexuality, Montana and Monty Python; Bob O'Neill (you remember: the OB-GYN from Rhode Island whom I first meet at the airport), who continues to be as sweet-natured and affable a physician as I've ever met; Ron Goldberg, a cardiologist from San Diego who turns out to be my doubles partner, frequent companion at the bar (and still a good friend), and virtual fountain of atherosclerotic information, answering a non-stop barrage of questions concerning my three heart operations, the combined efficacy of Zocor, niacin, and Colestid, and the internal structures of the RCA, the LAD, and the Circumflex; and Howard Rogg, a London solicitor who shares with me the painful saga of his prostate operation (mine is enlarged, plus I'm *still* in the act of trying to pass that kidney stone!) and against whom I will play a marathon singles match.

Then there are the pros. Now, I'm sure that there are celebrated athletes in all sports who are perfectly nice people. But all these famous guys, *without exception*, are terrific human beings! Maybe it's the Aussie brand of sportsmanship (which I've admired since I was a kid) that mixes fun, cajoling, and an intense competitive fire with a profound respect for the game, including its practitioners of yester-year. Furthermore, their games are still, after all these years, absolutely awesome. But more important, they all seem to be incredibly down-to-earth, warm, friendly, accessible, empathetic, enthusiastic, bright, and fun to be with; and they spend a great deal of time coaching, teaching, supporting, and kibitzing with the campers. In fact, since they appear to be enjoying themselves as much as anyone else, they *are* campers themselves! (The fact that their vocabulary is often punc-tuated by expressions that are in turn regurgitative, fecal, eructative, rectal, fornicative, penile, scrotal, macromastic, and callipygous serves as epoxy to the male bonding process.)

I'll begin with Ken Rosewall ("Muscles"). My childhood idol. I'm basically in awe of Muscles, more so than of anyone else. Not because he's the model athlete (modest to a fault, lets his actions speak for themselves, well-spoken, doesn't swear, clean-cut, appears to have no vices, amazing work ethic), but because his career is peerless: he was a *major* player in his sport for over a quarter of a century, win-ning, for example, U.S. championships fourteen years apart ('56, '70) and appearing in the finals ('74) at the age of nearly forty. I'm amazed and excited to be speaking with him casually at the bar the first night. We discuss his win over Hoad in the '56 U.S. finals to spoil Lew's Grand-Slam bid, the career of Mo Connolly (maybe the great-est female player ever), Slazenger racquets. I ask him how good Hoad really was. His response: "Aw, Liew's gyme, when it was awn, whenee troyed, he c'd d'fyte the lot of 'em. Whenee din't troy, anyone c'd d'fyte 'im." *Awesome!*

Cliff Drysdale ("Cliffie"), native of the Transvaal, is an authentic piece of work. One of the most brilliant speakers I've ever heard: glib, verbose, bombastic, colorful, caustic, vitriolic. His style is a mixture of British wit and erudition with American crudeness and scatology. Sort of a cross between George Bernard Shaw and Henry Miller. At one dinner, I laugh so hard at a peroration he delivers that I wish I'd brought along a box of Depends, if you get my drift. An example of a conversation (I think) we had at the bar one evening: *Me*: "So, Cliffie, I was at the U.S. finals in '65 when you lost to Santana. Helluva match!" *Cliffie*: "You were? Well, that ★★★★ was ★★★★ lucky that day. He hit so many ★★★★ lines, chalk was comin' out of his ★★★★★hole!" Yep, Cliffie was definitely the life of the party!

Roy Emerson ("Emmo") is, as my mother might say, a real gem. He combines Muscles' empathetic decency and Cliffie's caustic ribbing. Watching him play, you see why he won more Grand Slam titles than any other man in history: he still has the quick hands and the timing. There are two moments Emmo gives me during the week that I'll keep with me for a long time. The first occurs at the conclusion of my marathon singles match (more on that later). After shaking hands with my opponent, I collapse at the net as a result of the pain emanating from my injured right leg. Emmo (the coach of my *opponent!*) takes the time to ask me how I am, to chat with me for a moment, then to let me hang on him all the way to the gazebo, to sit me down so the trainer can work on me, and—to top it off—to fetch me an ice-cold Foster's! And all this from an immortal who had captured twenty-eight Grand Slam titles! The second moment results in a bit of knowledge he passes on to me that further widens my tennis ken. One day, I ask him how the hell he always used to keep his hair so immaculately (and maddeningly) in place. To which he replies, "Why, simple, myte: *Brylcream!*"

Marty Riessen is arguably the best athlete of the lot. In fact, he's not only one of the greatest American stars ever, but he also played college hoops for Northwestern. The first day of camp, I present him with a picture I had xeroxed from Zander Hollander's *The Modern Encyclopedia of Basketball*: Cazzie Russell (as a Michigan undergrad) is driving toward the basket, guarded by an athletic-looking, svelte Northwestern defender that looks suspiciously like Marty. For all these years, I had thought it was he, but I wasn't positive. It was: Marty confirms his identity and accepts the photo graciously. The two things I'll remember about Marty are, first, how bright and articulate he is. But then, having received his diploma from Northwestern (an athlete who actually finishes his degree, and at one of the toughest schools in the nation at that!), *no du-uh*, as my daughters would say. And second, the fact that Marty and I are undefeated as a doubles team (something he can't say about any other partner, even The Flying Dutchman, Tom Okker!).

Fred Stolle ("Fiery Fred"), like Cliffie, is incredibly outgoing, affable, and possesses a ready and caustic wit. His game (these days) is deceptive: despite his avuncular appearance, he's a viper on the court, waiting in the weeds and then striking without warning with quick hands and savvy. Fred, I think, has the most fun of all the pros, or so it seems, and he never misses an opportunity to retaliate. Case in point: the first day, I tell Fiery that I've gone to every U.S. championship since 1951, with the exception of '66 (the year he won it). I apologize quasi-abjectly, we laugh and leave it at that. That evening, as he's presenting me with the "Charlie Hustle" Award at dinner, before maybe 100 people including my peers and all the pros and the kitchen staff, he takes great pleasure in mentioning the little chat we had that morning, then proceeds to insult me, my girlfriend, my sexual habits, and virtually everything I stand for and hold sacred in this world.

Mal Anderson, appropriately, is the only pro who doesn't have a nickname. Maybe it's because there are no frills or façades to this pleasant man from Queensland. Just Mal. He's one of our team's coaches and is a true testimony to the notion that really decent people can succeed at the highest level of sports. Mal is a great guy, tremendously supportive, gracious, self-deprecating. After injuring my leg the second day, I mention to him somewhat flippantly that I feel like Ashley Cooper in the '58 U.S. final (Cooper beat him that year despite a bum leg). Instead of bristling, he laughs pleasantly and lets it go. I dunno, maybe in his private life Mal is a homicidal maniac and tortures kittens and puppies. But on the outside, he's as sweet a guy as you're ever gonna meet.

Charlie Pasarell is down-to-earth, articulate, fun to talk to. The first night, I'm with him at the bar (where else?), and I'm impressed by how forthcoming he is. We talk about lots of stuff, some pretty private. I learn that he's got a daughter at Princeton, that he's got deep family values, that he's a damn good businessman/entrepreneur. The one moment I'll remember about Charlie has to do with his coaching. My first singles match, I'm playing a tall guy who's about 6'9". (Since I am 5'7" myself, anyone over 5'9" is tall.) I'm playing out of my mind the first set, which I win, 6–1. The second set, Bill's serve suddenly kicks in. He's serving like Colin Dibley or Mike Sangster or Goran Ivanisevic at their best: 130 mph, hitting the lines, acing me at least two or three times every service game. (Plus I can't push off of my injured right leg, to boot!) Anyway, he's got me, 5–1, and it sure looks like it's heading fast into a third set. So Charlie, who's watching all this, strolls behind me as Bill gets set to serve a new game. He says, without fanfare, "Stand six feet behind the baseline." To which I respond, "But I rely on my reflexes for the return, so I'm more comfortable at the baseline." He asks, "What's the score?" I answer, "5–1, his." To which Charlie peremptorily orders me, *"Do it!"* So I stand back six feet, start returning Bill's serve, break him, crawl back into the set, and before I know it, I take the next six games for the match: 6–1, 7–5. Good ol' Charlie!

The two guys I never really get a chance to know are Owen Davidson ("Davo") and Tony Roche ("Rochie"). Maybe it's because they're a bit more reserved than some of the other guys, or maybe there's just a limit as to how many opportunities come up in six days. Anyway, my point about these two is that neither needs to speak to be heard. Their games are still so impressive that I learn a great deal just watching. "Davo," the more jocular of the two (he's in charge of "hooking" speakers during dinnertime orations: when they get too obnoxious or verbose, he snags 'em with a giant white shepherd's crook), is regarded as the greatest mixed-doubles player ever. And you can see why. He's incredible during the exhibition matches, with uncanny reflexes and court sense. I pick up lots of strategy watching him hit and move around the court. I'll basically remember "Rochie" from a clinic he gives one morning on the backhand volley. (If anyone, past or present, has a better one, let him come forth now!) With Muscles hitting backhands to him at the net, Rochie knocks off one after the other, with authority and uncanny accuracy. "Y'mus' myke a ply by turnin' y'showlda an' hittin' aowt!," he barks. *Yes, sir!*

I've saved Newk for last. I guess because he's really the grease that makes the wheels turn (or whatever the metaphor is). The ultimate showman, Newk makes all the campers feel right at home (it's *his*, after all). Like Charlie and Mal, he also coaches our team, and he's always there to give support, advice, and solace. The first day of team practice, we're hitting: what I find so impressive is the speed with which he can size up your game. Not more than twenty seconds into the rally, he tells me I need to get more shoulder turn into my backhand. Precisely the defect I've been working on for the past thirty years! The greatest pleasure, though, that I extract from my interaction with Newk has to do with trivia. We hurl each other daunting, esoteric trivia grenades continuously, some of them during "rap sessions" in front of great crowds of people, one attempting to maim the other (or at least to mortify him deeply). Druck, my ally, is also heavily involved in the attacks. I must admit that Newk is pretty amazing: he knows virtually everything about tennis, past and present. He knows the scores of matches forty years ago, the sites of Davis Cup ties, the fact that Sirola was Pietrangeli's doubles partner and that Clark Graebner had a little jump-hitch when he served. So stumping him is no easy task. Druck and I pepper him constantly during the first four days, trying to fatigue him, to break his will. Newk is a fighter, a champion, though: we know this. But finally, our persistence and dogged aggression take their toll. As Newk reels with mental fatigue from the Yankee onslaught, I deliver the fatal knockout blow in the form of two dazzlingly esoteric queries: "Was Carol Fageros the most attractive female player ever?" (He's never even *heard* of her!) And "Who, man or woman, were the only two people to win all twelve Grand Slam events for which their sex was eligible?" (Actually, none of the pros can name the second one. Newk and many others get Margaret Court, but Doris Hart eludes them all!) At any rate, Newk is, like all the other pros, just a great guy, gracious and eminently accessible.

What's particularly gratifying is seeing all these guys close up. I mean, I'd seen them all play many times over the years and was well acquainted with their mannerisms on the court and their professional personae in front of the camera. But observing what's inside their hearts and brains and how they care for us campers and for one another is very special indeed.

So much for the celestial *dramatis personae*. But heaven is, of course, more than just the people inhabiting it, which begs two questions. What's the typical heavenly day like? And what's the greatest lesson learned there, the most enduring memory?

The days in Paradise seem virtually endless. They are filled—no, crammed—wall-to-wall with things *tennis*. For a tennis nut, it's unreal! You get up, shower, and go to breakfast: a sumptuous buffet of everything from eggs and sausages to (for those of us who are cholesterol-conscious) granola and yogurt. You scarf up a big plate of whatever and sit down at one of the twenty-odd long tables, at which are likely to be three or four campers and a pro or two. You talk to Muscles or Mal about a '54 Davis Cup match or a '57 Grand Slam final, or ask Emmo who his toughest opponent was, or get some tips from Marty or Charlie about the half-volley.

Then you hobble through fifteen minutes of calisthenics with Larry Starr, who for twenty-five years was the trainer for the Cincinnati Reds and (currently) the Florida Marlins. Then there's a clinic from one of the pros: Charlie on the half-volley, Rochie on the backhand volley, Fiery on the forehand drive. Then the competitive matches begin. We're all divided into four teams: The Musclemen (coached, obviously, by Muscles, plus Rochie and Davo), The Wankers (Aussie for "jerk-offs" and coached by Emmo and Marty), The Dunnies (Aussie for "outhouses" and coached by Cliffie and Fiery), and The Lawnmowers (coached by Mal, Charlie, and Newk, who coined the name: "You're a Lawnmower, 'cause your ass is grass!"). There are usually singles matches in the A.M., dubs in the P.M.: the matches this year are all incredibly close and hotly contested. It's great fun to watch everyone cheering for their "mytes" and all the pros coaching their hearts out, not only for bragging rights but for pride (they don't screw around when it comes to competition, which explains why they're among the greatest players ever). Between singles and doubles matches, there's either an exhibition doubles match featuring four of the pros or a rap session or drills with the ranch pros or some other tennis-related activity. Next comes lunch, where you feast on some delectable culinary offering and chat with pros and campers about . . . yep, tennis! Then the doubles matches. Then the "fantasy matches," which pit camper and pro against camper and pro. One set, for all the marbles! Then your own personal massage and a pre-dinner shower. Then happy hour, held in the bar (the "Billabong"), where the wonderful and gracious Cassie serves you a

Foster's or a single-malt scotch and you chew the fat with campers and pros about . . . guess what.

Dinner is about the most heavenly of all the heavenly events of the day. It is loud, raucous, spirited, filled with surprises, speeches, insults, male bonding, and lively conversation. The fare is wonderful: one night pasta, crustacea the next, washed down with endless bottles of exquisite wine from California, Australia, and Texas. (Wine from *Texas???!!*) Cliffie usually stands up and entertains the troops for five or ten minutes. Davo tries to give him the hook, and an ugly altercation ensues. Then Newk and Emmo and Cliffie and some of the other "legends" hurl insults across the room, with a bunch of us campers getting into the act. A highlight of every dinner is the presentation of two daily awards. The "Horse's Ass" Award is presented to the guy who had acted particularly egregiously that day. He's presented with an honest-to-God (plastic) equine rump, complete with polyester tail, which he's compelled to tie around his waist and wear (except during matches) until dinner on the following eve, when he passes it on to the subsequent recipient. Then there's the "Wanker" Award, given to the "dickhead of the day." He's presented with a similar trophy: a polyurethane penile-head hat under which he's resigned to parade the entire next day! At dinner, there are also analytical discussions of today's tennis vs. yesterday's, the changes in equipment, etc., as well as war stories told at the podium by the pros about Davis Cup or Grand Slam matches of yore, complete with the appropriate drama and hyperbole. My favorite is Muscles' description of his boyhood idol, Jack Bromwich, who used to play (late thirties through early fifties) with a tiny (eleven-ounce) racquet shaved to a tiny butt at the end, strung at twenty-five pounds! He was very unorthodox, with a lefty serve, righty forehand, and two-handed backhand. Once, his racquet (the same one he had kept for seven years!) popped a string during a match against the great Lew Hoad. Brom simply tied the string up manually and proceeded to win!

Following dinner, all us tennis nuts tromp into the bar again, drink till the wee hours, sing some karaoke, talk about . . . (well, you know by now), then drag ourselves back to our condos, every bone and muscle in our bodies aching, where we collapse in our respective beds, our brains soon filled with visions of all the wonderful tennis that will take place on the morrow.

And what's the most enduring lesson/memory I leave heaven with? It has to do with the injury I sustain, and it's maybe the best part. In fact, as soon as I pass through these pearly gates, I begin to realize how all those dumb clichés we grow up with are so true. *Hey, you never know. There are no roses without thorns. In every cloud, there's a silver lining. No pain, no gain. In the kingdom of the blind, the one-eyed are kings.* The week is filled with surprises, challenges, and obstacles; and I'm amazed at how much I learn not only about tennis, but about myself and people in general.

The saga all starts on the second day, during Lawnmower team practice. As I stretch to retrieve a drop shot, I feel a familiar pull in the upper calf of my right leg. I've torn it before, but as I feel it rip, a groan of disappointment struggles up my throat, then subsides. Resigned to five days of mediocre, disappointing tennis at one-quarter strength (that Jewish paranoia thing again), I limp to the gazebo to get some medical treatment. The trip seems to take hours. (I imagine I am Ralph Branca dragging himself to the clubhouse after delivering up the infamous gopher ball to Bobby Thomson. . . .) Bad, nasty thoughts are creeping into my head. *Oh no. I finally get through two recent heart operations, all the back pain, the kidney stone, the scorpion sting, and now this! My dream of a lifetime is going up in smoke, before my very eyes, and I'm gonna end up playing like Chester from Gunsmoke!*

Well, all I can say is, thank God for Larry Starr (the trainer). Larry is basically The Wizard of Tape and Healing. What he can accomplish with his hands and bandages and electronic equipment and salves is nothing short of miraculous. So he tapes me up from ankle to knee, applies ice every hour, puts on tons of Flexall 454 ("hot stuff"), and zaps the muscle with a huge dose of electrical current. He is a modern-day Dr. Frankenstein, I his beloved and grateful monster. In fact, after thinking at first that I was done for, I now feel my confidence on the rise, and I know I'm gonna be able to give it a go. My adrenaline is flowing big-time, my desire is febrile. Funny thing is, as much as it still hurts, it really doesn't matter if I win or lose my matches, as long as I can compete and not let my team down. That's what it's all about here. In fact, nothing could happen (short of a *truly* crippling injury) that could ever spoil this experience.

As things turn out, my leg ends up getting worse every day. On the third day, Ron Goldberg and I play a marathon doubles match, which we lose, 6–7, 5–7. I'm limping around like Quasimodo, he's covering two-thirds of the court, the swirling winds are Candlestick-quality, and we're playing the strong team of Bob O'Neill and the 6'9" Bill Druckemiller (you'll remember him from my singles match), who's awesome at net and seems like he's 8'13". But we're both enjoying the hell out of this living-nightmare-of-a-match: as it is the last one of the morning (it lasts well over two hours), all the other members of the Lawnmowers and Dunnies assemble to watch, cheering on their respective teammates, giving support and encouragement, and appreciating the competitive tennis being played and the intense effort being put forth. (How else would people behave in heaven?) We're giving it 120%, as we run into fences, tumble into water-coolers, and earn every inch of our "Charlie Hustle" Awards! (One of my somersaults results in a slight pull of the mid-hamstring of my right leg, and after the match, I pay one of my ten-a-days to my good buddy Larry. I am now taped from ankle to mid-thigh.)

In the afternoon, I drag my bionic taped-and-iced-and-electrified leg to my singles match, where—*oh no!*—the 6'9" Bill is hungrily awaiting me. (Our opponents are unknown to us until the matches actually begin.) He now seems like he's about 13'23"! You know how this match ends (Charlie's classic tip), but you should also know that I pull another muscle (in my upper hammie this time), and compared to mine, Chester's limp would be virtually undetectable. Following Larry's tape job that afternoon, which now extends from ankle to groin, I am affectionately referred to as "The Mummy."

Which brings us to my singles match of the next day, against "The Human Backboard," Howard Rogg (the prostateless London solicitor). To make a *very* long story short, *we play a two-set match in a little under three hours and fifteen minutes!* Because I can't move around at all, I try to beat him at his own game: all I'm hitting are moonballs and dropshots. I'm ahead in the first set, 5–3, I have him all figured out, and I'm well on my way to pulling off an heroic victory. But no! As Fate would have it, I pull yet another small muscle at fifteen-love, and I know deep inside that it's all over right then and there. I end up losing the match, but not without a dogged fight: nearly every game goes to deuce, some to ten or twelve deuces! After the final point, I am completely, utterly spent: the pain shooting through my leg feels like an admixture of childbirth, coronary infarction, and kidney stones moving around in the ureter. But it doesn't matter at all that I lose: all that matters is that I give it my best shot. It also feels exhilarating to dig deep down inside when things seem utterly hopeless and see what resources are available and willing to be used. Further, the match bonds Howard and me even more than before (beyond our common prostate problems) and allows Emmo to demonstrate his aforementioned empathy and humanity. I'm not surprised: that's the kind of thing that happens routinely here in The Great Beyond.

As it turns out, I win my last two matches: a team doubles match on the fifth day and my "fantasy match" on the final morning, which is a real treat, sort of icing on the cake. Marty and I beat Emmo and another camper, 6–4. All I remember from the match (besides barely being able to limp around) are three winners I hit: two on the first two points of the match (sharply angled volley, deadened underspin dropshot), plus a scorching forehand down Emmo's alley after I warn him digitally—just as Ruth did prior to his famous homer in that '32 Series game at Wrigley—of what I am about to perpetrate. *That* was one I'll tell my grandkids about. (P.S. Emmo takes it graciously, plus he and I know secretly that he probably could've gotten to it.)

After this final match, I droop onto a bench in the gazebo and drape a towel over my head. My body is racked, my leg throbbing. But my heart and soul and spirits are in another realm, one they sometimes refer to as "beatitude." I am totally, gloriously filled with the joy of having given my last proverbial gasp to a game I love. I couldn't possibly hit another tennis ball, even if someone were to threaten me with having to eat a bowl of Brussels sprouts if I didn't.

By now, it's noontime, and all that's left of this heavenly week is to say good-bye to all my new friends, campers and pros alike. What a six days it has been! Despite my aches and pains, I'm smiling ear to ear. And as everyone departs (I decide to stay another day to lick my wounds and get some massage therapy), I muse about how there'd be no more wars or misery in the world if all us humans could share common passions (like tennis) and treat one another with the same respect and empathy as those campers and legends did during that transcendental Texas interlude in the mid-autumn of 1996.

So basically, that's how I spent my six days in heaven. Six unforgettable days that were exhilarating and exhausting, inspiring and tiring. Without a doubt, the six most incredible, indelible, energizing, enervating, challenging, punishing, wearing, tearing, grueling, refueling days I've ever spent in my entire life.

And on the seventh day, I rested.

How to Name Your Dog

I don't know about you, but I've always wondered why otherwise perfectly intelligent people would name their dogs Rover or Rex or Spot or Fido or Fluffy or Muffy or Missy or Nippy or Happy or Lucky or Red or Biff or Penny or Pal or Rusty or Skippy or Taffy or Blackie. I mean, giving a dog a name that's either obvious ("O.K., I get it, he's black!") or timeworn ("Oh no, not another *Rusty!*") seems to me the ultimate missed opportunity, the surrendering of the precious privilege to do something—*one thing!*—in life that would be purely creative and personal and unique and individualistic.

As far as I'm concerned, any self-respecting dog oughta have a name that *means* something to its owner. On a visceral level. I mean, besides the creativity issue, the fact of the matter is that you're gonna be calling their name somewhere in the neighborhood of thirty to forty million times, from the time they're a puppy till the moment they draw their final gasp, so it *better* have very special meaning!

So, pursuant to my theory concerning canine nomenclature, I put some real quality time into naming *my* special pal before I pick him up at the breeder's farm.

For starters, I spend a few hours in the Sonoma Public Library looking into the history of the Hottentots and their language. (At this point, you're probably asking—and rightfully so—why in the world I'm doing research on the Hottentots and, even more to the point, what the hell a "doggie" story is doing in this collection of sports essays.) You see, the breed I've selected is the Rhodesian Ridgeback, a proud, loyal dog originally bred by the Hottentots of Rhodesia (now Zimbabwe) to track down and corner lions. (*Aha!*) After making a list of names and expressions of Hottentot origin (e.g.,"khoikhoin"), nothing particularly clicks. In my mind, I hear my voice calling out to the little rascal (*Here, khoikhoin!*) or reprimanding him (*Bad khoikhoin!*). But the experiment proves fruitless, as my instincts are left cold and unimpressed.

Coming to my senses, I leave the sterile academic confines of the library and return home to ponder my dilemma. *Let's see, what kind of name would speak to me more personally? What arena of interest do I really, really care about?* And then, suddenly, as it always does, the cartoon electric light bulb flickers on in the thought balloon directly above my head. Aha! Eureka! Of course! I'll give him a name from the world of *sports*, a name that's intensely significant to me, that has emotional resonance, that *means* something when I beckon to, scold, or reward him!

The next step in the process involves flipping through all the appealing, meaningful, dog-appropriate names in the long and storied history of organized athletics—sport by painstaking sport—that happen to be stored, stashed, piled up, catalogued, or hidden in my cerebral lobes and fissures. (If the ideal name isn't somewhere in my brain, I figure, it can't have any deep or symbolic meaning.)

O.K. Starting with tennis, I'm first struck by the irony that perhaps my two favorite names in this sport have to be eliminated right off the bat (or in this case, the racquet). One, "Molla" (as in Molla Mallory), is unfortunately a girl's name (my puppy is a male); the other, the first name of one of my favorite Aussie Davis Cup players ("Rex" Hartwig), has an obvious fatal flaw. But not to worry: the history of tennis has bequeathed to us a large number of colorful, even flamboyant names from which to choose. Racquing my brain, I come up with a worthy list of finalists: Muscles, Mervyn, Alejandro, Onny, Mats, Gottfried, Budge, Jaroslav, Nicola, Tappy, Manolo, Ilie, Björn, Ellsworth, Ashley, Pancho, Yannick, and, naturally, my personal favorite, Ramanathan.

Golf is a bit less charitable in terms of its repertoire of colorful and canine-friendly names. But still, I cull from its midst: Horton, Byron, Fuzzy, Seve, Jose-Maria, Chi Chi, Kel, Dow, Payne, Lawson, Julius, Hubert, Duffy, and (the front-runner) Orville.

Hockey, likewise, is somewhat frugal. To my liking, the only authentic hockey names are, with a few notable exceptions, French ones. So, for finalists, I'm going with: Marcel, Jacques, Jean, Guy, Henri, Maurice, Denis, Gilbert, Yvan, Michel, and that favorite of Gallic hockey fans, Boom Boom. (I'll also add to the mix: Turk, Gump, Gordie, and, *bien sûr*, The Great One.)

It gets better.

Football "dog names" abound, but I have to be selective. So I narrow down my votes for serious consideration to: Yelberton, Big Daddy, Night Train, Deacon Dan, Ozzie, Lionel, MacArthur, Greasy, Bronco, Tobin, Boomer, Kellen, Cookie, Franco, Preston, Ottis, Herschel, Babe, Roman, Ollie, Abner, Stump, Cloyce, Crazylegs, Curly, Too Tall, Ahmad, Dub, Weeb, and (my dark horse) Uwe.

Then there's the basketball arena, proffering these memorable monikers: Easy Ed, Clyde the Glide, Wilt the Stilt, Nate the Skate,

Dolph, Kareem, Hakeem, Elgin, Elvin, Isiah, Dr. J., Pistol Pete, Magic, Dominique, Spencer, Moses, Micheal Ray, Swen, World B., Artis, Cotton, and The Big O. Now tell me honestly, what proud dog-owners wouldn't want to select one of these noble names for their pooches?

Which brings us to baseball. Ah, baseball! I know deep down that this is the sport from which I'll most likely choose my puppy's name, I guess because it's always been, in a certain sense, the sport closest to my heart. Anyway, the baseball list of great doggy names is truly impressive and voluminous. And after a good deal of pondering, ratiocinating, and juggling, I finally cut my list of finalists down to a scant forty: Satchel, Virgil, Peanuts, Vinegar Bend, Alpha, Early, Cuno, Hoot, Coot, Cot, Spec, Ike, Suitcase, Minnie, Camillo, Ferris, Bo, Bobo, Bubba, Ebba, Dusty, Shotgun, Suitcase, Granny, Dee, Pumpsie, Choo Choo, Ryne, Puddin' Head, Rip, Reno, Del, Galen, Ewell, Enos, Solly, Chico, Ossie, Spook, and, naturally, Sibby.

The penultimate act, before the actual final choice is made, is to incubate. So I make a huge list of all these worthy finalists, tape it to my computer, and study it. For days, I turn the names around in my skull, taking each one individually and calling it out aloud with my inner (dog-owner's) voice: *Here, Ramanathan! Bad boy, Orville! Heel, The Great One! Fetch, Night Train! Down, Micheal Ray! Come, Vinegar Bend!*

For some reason, no matter which name I use with these hypothetical commands, nothing works. No epithet succeeds in striking an instinctual chord within the deepest part of me. And suddenly, I am struck with terror, with the ultimate, most ineffable horror of all.

Will my puppy go nameless his entire life?

I have sickening visions of my calling the little tyke, amidst a crowd of curious onlookers, mortified by the palpable absence of his canine identity: *Here, ... !*

But then, as so often happens in life just as the present situation seems bleakest, I experience an epiphany, a sudden and illogical vision that appears in my head. It is a doggy name that is perfect, a doggy name that is ideal! And not only that, it's accompanied by the Topps baseball card of the player whose name has been sent down to me by God knows what celestial power. It's the name—and the card—of my all-time-favorite-player-with-a-name-that's-perfect-for-a-dog.

MAGLIE!!!!!!!!!!!

Of course: how could I not have seen it? Right there under my nose! Maglie! I know in my deepest depths that it's right, this most perfect of all doggy names! Yet something in me, perhaps the very human desire to savor one's good fortune (the Yiddish word is *kvell*), compels me to sit on my laurels, to analyze my choice, to let myself, as Browning (Liz, not Tom) might have said, "count the ways."

To begin with, Salvatore Anthony Maglie was, with the possible exception of Willie Howard Mays, my favorite ballplayer of all time. I just loved the guy! Ironically, I grew up in Brooklyn a die-hard New York Giants fan. (My father's older sister was a Yankee fan, so he *had* to be a Giants fan, which predilection was passed down to me genetically.) And in the early fifties, the Giants had a great run, winning two pennants in four years ('51, '54). Sal Maglie was the mainstay of a very good Giants pitching staff, but what was it about him that I found so appealing? What made him so worthy of being chosen as the namesake of my loyal, adorable puppy?

Certainly not because he was loyal or adorable! He didn't get along particularly with the Giants' management and went on to play for the Indians, Dodgers, Yankees, and Cardinals. (He was, in fact, the last human being to play for all three New York baseball teams.) And adorable? After Don Mossi, Sal had the least adorable face of any baseball player ever. But still, there was something about his look that I found appealing. Perhaps the fact that it was so . . . *hang-dog*?

No, I loved Maglie first of all because of his fiercely competitive nature. I mean, he didn't take any crap from *nobody*! (You want that trait in a dog: independence, strength, self-confidence.) He never backed down from a challenge and always wanted to be in command. Which is why they called him "The Barber": his "brush-back" pitch was renowned, the nasty curve high and tight that would compose "chin music" and tell the batter exactly who was boss. (Which, parenthetically, brings to mind one of the great quotes of all time, uttered by Tito Fuentes, the Puerto Rican second baseman of the Giants of the sixties. When asked about "beanball" pitchers, Tito responded: "They shouldn't throw at me. I'm the father of five or six children.") Anyway, Sal's frequent and intensely combative confrontations with Jackie Robinson, one of the other great competitors of all time, are legend.

Then there was his work ethic. (You want your dog to be a hard worker, to know the value of labor.) Maglie was definitely blue-collar all the way. The son of poor immigrants, Sal was born and raised in the lower-class Italian section of Niagara Falls. He always had it tough, and his baseball career reflects this struggle: spending long years plying his trade in Canada and Mexico and forced out of the Giants' rotation as a result of politics, he finally made it to the majors on a full-time basis in 1950, at the tender age of thirty-three!

What's even more amazing about Maglie, despite the late start and the bad breaks, was his actual pitching ability. (In addition to having that doggy look and being independent and hard-working, your pooch should be extremely *able* in his performance of tricks, fetching sticks and stuff, guarding your life and property, and getting your slippers.) Dare I say that Sal Maglie had one of the most remarkable pitching careers in the history of organized baseball? (*Sal Maglie?*) Yep, starting in earnest at the ripe-old age of thirty-three, Sal compiled a lifetime record of 119–62, for a winning percentage of .657, one of the best ever. Even more spectacular was his *start* in the majors. In his first three full years (not counting his first, "partial" year of 1945), he was 18–4, 23–6, and 18–8, for a total of 59–18 (.766).

Now let's put that in perspective by comparing him to seven of the greatest pitchers in baseball history, in terms of their records for their first three full years (not counting the first, "incomplete" year, where applicable):

> Walter Johnson: 52–56 (.481)
> Bob Gibson: 31–31 (.500)
> Sandy Koufax: 24–21 (.533)
> Christy Mathewson: 63–47 (.573)
> Warren Spahn: 57–36 (.613)
> Grover Cleveland Alexander: 69–38 (.645)
> Cy Young: 98–48 (.671)
> **Sal Maglie: 59–18 (.766)**

Maglie simply had the best winning percentage (by a mere 95 points!), the fewest losses, and—except for the prodigious trio of Young, Alexander, and Mathewson—the most wins during that period. Imagine the records he might've held had he begun his career at the age of nineteen!

(Did you also realize that near the end of his career, in 1956 *at the age of thirty-nine*, Maglie pitched a no-hitter against the Phillies and also lost that perfect World Series game thrown by Don Larsen, in which Sal himself pitched a five-hitter and gave up but two runs?)

On top of all this, Maglie had one of the great curveballs ever (developed in the high altitudes of Mexico), was tireless, never whined, and almost always came up big in the crucial games. I can still see him in my loving mind's eye, standing on the mound, snarling at the batter, shaking off the fastball sign given by Wes Westrum, and breaking off yet another mean, tantalizing curve that shaves the inside corner.

And the icing on the cake: as if all this love and affection for the ballplayer whose name is now eternally affixed to my pooch weren't enough, the plain truth of the matter is that I also simply adore the name itself. It is euphonic, pithy, and rolls trippingly off the tongue. Try it yourself, if you don't believe me: *Here, Maglie! Come, Maglie! Stay, Maglie! Down, Maglie! Fetch, Maglie! Bad boy, Maglie! Good boy, Maglie!*

Break off that nasty curve high and tight, Maglie!!!

Wallball!

Every time that first delectable smell of spring comes wafting through the air, what does it make you think of? The beginning of the baseball season? Romance? Planting the annuals? Cleaning out your closets? For me, all of these come to mind, but what I always think of *first* is the memory of a very special ritual that once symbolized all that is beautiful, renewing, and innocent about this season, and still does.

Wallball!

I swear, it's always like clockwork: first smell of spring, *wallball!* Like a page right out of Proust, where a particular scent immediately and magically elicits a vivid and specific memory attached to it.

The setting is Williams College, which in 1966 was an all-men's (there are now, mercifully, women gracing its student body) liberal-arts college in the "Purple Valley" of the Berkshires in northwestern Massachusetts.

It is my senior year, second semester, and life couldn't be more idyllic if it tried. My plans to teach in France the following fall are all set; there's no pressure, since grades don't mean zippo any more. The air is replete with the bounties of floral perfume: lilac, wisteria, honeysuckle. I fill my nostrils to the brim, slo-mo, like Ferdinand the Bull sniffing his posies. I am lying on the roof—so the memory goes—of Philip Spencer House (née Chi Psi), a copy of Baudelaire in one hand, a glass of suds from the house keg in the other. Dogs are in heat all over the campus, and letting off proverbial steam. Yep, spring has sprung, and if you close your eyes up there, all you can hear are the sounds of underclassmen bantering on their way to a seminar, a record (yes, a *record!*) of Dusty Springfield or Little Eva, bees pollenating, canines copulating. It's as close to heaven as you're gonna get.

And then, as if it's the official trumpeting of spring, a stentorian shout drifts up from below.

Wallball!

And rousting ourselves from our reveries, happy to interrupt them for this maddest of all sporting rituals, are The Faithful Eight. Atlas. Corbin. Kramer. Mitchell. Moore. Nesvig. Straub. Williamson. Proudly wearing the uniforms of the sport (shorts, and not a stitch else), we align ourselves on the court, ready to greet the season of renewal and, at long last, bid adieu to the harshness of winter.

The court is, officially, the half of the porch to the left of the front door of the former frat house; the tools are an old tennis ball and your palms. The game is sort of like squash or handball but really neither: it has rules and an etiquette and a spirit that are peculiarly its own.

Here's the deal. You start the point by hitting the ball, on a bounce, against the front wall. Each guy has a number in the order. The ball has to hit the front wall, then bounce, and before it bounces twice, the next guy has to hit it back to the front wall on one bounce, and so on. Until one guy can't get to the ball on one bounce. If not, he gets a point and goes to the end of the order. (The prime location is to serve, or be #1.) Three points, you're out. Until there's two guys left, and then whoever gets three, the other guy wins.

Sound simple? Hold your horses.

You can get some amazing angles and force other players into some incredible predicaments. There's a flower bed, for instance, behind the playing area, into which, if you hit the ball sufficiently deep, you send the next guy sprawling. The ideal shot is struck as you crouch way down (sort of like the "egg" position downhill skiers get into), then you slap the ball as low as possible, approaching parallel, so that it barely goes more than an inch or so from ground level. It thus scuttles along, ideally to the next guy's backhand (i.e., *left* hand if he's a righty), forcing him to make a diving, unnatural left-handed shot. You can get some incredible angles, as I said, so the point stretches out way beyond the length of the front wall. Guys go flying into flowers, smashing into walls, slaloming around other guys to get to the ball or to avoid contact, flailing and diving all over the place, scraping elbows, cursing, screaming. I mean, how much fun, and how exciting, can athletic competition get? I've gotta say that although I played three sports in college (soccer, squash, tennis), I never felt the surge of violent passion and competitive juices as much as I did playing this one.

Wallball!

I mean, this game had everything. Excitement. Competitive fervor. Fun. But on top of all this, it demanded the gamut of athletic skills. Power. Timing. Finesse. Strategy. Brains. Conditioning. Flexibility. You also developed an amazing repertoire of shots, each devilishly employed at the appropriate time: right- and left-handed "scuttle" shots, flat shots, slap shots, angles, drop shots, topspin, underspin, sidespin, lunges, behind-the-backers, through-the-leggers.

But wait a sec: there's more!

Besides all this good stuff, there was the incredible camaraderie that developed, mostly because of the game's etiquette. As vicious and unrelenting as the competition got, there was always a sense of fairness and excruciating adherence to the game's written-in-stone rules. We all knew the boundaries of the court, what shots were or weren't permit-

ted (e.g., "carries," "two-bouncers"), and which blocks and body contact were or weren't illegal. If you bumped another guy, for instance, a
collective yell would fill the air, ruling—jury-style in the manner of the
cards in *Alice in Wonderland*—that you had transgressed and had lost the
point. No argument. *To the end of the line with you!* As a result, we'd all
yell and scream and jostle and ridicule, but, in the spirit of what's best
about sporting competition, we all knew right from wrong and would
exquisitely abide by the rules and the collective ethics and wisdom of
the others.

A typical game would last, say, forty-five minutes. Or two hours.
Depending on how much beer we'd drunk and how long the friendly
rhubarbs went on. But let's call it an hour and a half.

An hour and a half of zaniness, craziness, fun, enjoyment, passion,
screaming, and competition. But most of all, it was an hour and a half
of FREEDOM. The kind of freedom that *any* sport at its finest gives a
body. With the added feature that we were young, and goofy, and fool-
ish, and unencumbered by the responsibilities and obligations with
which life would later burden us. And we all *knew* it, as we dived,
lunged, drank, kidded, ridiculed, and satisfied our sporting passions during those long, sweet sessions in the Purple Valley, amid the smells of
lilac and the sounds of rock 'n' roll and fornicating dogs.

And that, in a nutshell, is why—no matter where I am, or what
year it is, or what the situation, or how sweet or bitter life seems to be
at that moment—whenever I smell that first hint of spring, the very
first thing my mind wanders to isn't baseball or romance or petunia
seeds or spring cleaning. It's Atlas and Corbin and Kramer and Mitchell
and Moore and Nesvig and Straub and Williamson.

And *wallball!*

The Trouble with Soccer

So I was watching the final of the 1998 World Cup the other day. You know, *the* World Cup? It was an entrancing, exciting affair, full of emotion and drama and upset and surprise and ebb and flow, as all great sporting events should be. Featuring the valiant stifling by the Gallic defense (Lebœuf, Desailly, Lizarazu, et al.) of the brilliant Brazilian offensive machine (Denilson, Rivaldo, Ronaldo, et al.). The two dramatic first-half goals by the Algerian Zidane, both headers off corner kicks, both surprising and glorious and heart-breaking. The actual rekindling of a dormant national pride by a single victory, courtesy of the underdog and dogged host team. And suddenly, from out of the (French) blue, in the midst of all this electricity, I began to muse about what the trouble with soccer is.

I just said "the trouble with soccer," not "the trouble with football," because there is *no* trouble with the game of football, as the world outside of the U.S. uses this term and as far as I can see. I love football (theirs), played it in high school and college, followed the

English, French, Italian, German, Spanish, and Dutch leagues for years, understand the principles of the game, and appreciate its niceties and nuances and profound beauty. (More on that later.) But there are a number of flaws related to the game as we Americans perceive it (i.e., "soccer"), particularly as it relates to the relative popularity of football (ours) as a spectator sport. (Are you still with me?) And so, it's my judgment that at this point in the history of sport, a brief apologia for their football and a modest apology for ours is certainly in order.

To begin with, one of the troubles with soccer resides in the name itself. I suppose we couldn't call it football because the name was already taken by the sport of "American" (tackle) football. But the fact remains that in the U.S., soccer should really be called football, just as it's called in every other country on the planet. Why? Because every sport should be named after its most germane and definitive aspect. To wit: baseball is the only game played with bases as its main path of traffic. Stoopball is, uniquely and unlike any other sport, played against a stoop. The main goal of basketball is to shoot a ball into a, well, you get the picture. Likewise, football (theirs) is the only major sport played entirely without the use of hands, i.e., with the foot. It is, in a word . . . *foot*ball! On the other hand, football (ours) couldn't be farther from this concept and is, thus, the epitome of a misnomer. The only time a foot is used in *our* game is for punting and kicking field goals and extra points, which collective acts take up maybe one minute out of a total of sixty, or a little less than 2% of the entire game. Clearly, the game should be called something like "goalball," since what defines it is crossing the *goal* line. (P.S. if you're wondering where we got "soccer" from, it's basically an abbreviated form of "association football.")

Another trouble with soccer is the American (mis)perception of the game's dynamics. In the States, football (ours) is generally perceived by fans as a much more exciting, "action-packed" game than its worldwide namesake. But if you think about it for a minute (or even a second), you'll probably acknowledge that the truth may reside, let us say, elsewhere. Our football is basically: five or ten seconds of action (I use the term advisedly: it's sometimes nothing more than a stultifying, somnolent off-tackle play for no gain), followed by thirty seconds to a minute of rest and fallowness. In other words, while everyone is catching his breath (except for the impatient spectator), the non-action is transpiring, to the tune of maybe 88% of the game's elapsed time! By contrast, in *their* football, play is continuous. Non-stop. Perpetual motion. The clock keeps ticking (and the action continues), even when the ball is out of bounds, until the forty-five minutes of each half has expired, and even then, there's "stoppage time" (a continuation of play of anywhere between one and five minutes, to make up for the rare "stoppage" of play that occurs during goal-scoring and injuries). And we Americans, by and large (and mostly due to our ignorance of the nuances), consider football (theirs) to be a dull affair!

In short, the trouble with soccer, with our country's perception of the game, is that we are missing out on what makes it so wonderful as a sport—on aspects of the game that are absent, or perhaps only partially present, in our "more exciting" brand of football. Four of these attributes, undoubtedly among many others, immediately spring to mind and need to be brought at once to our collective national consciousness.

One: it has *flow*. Because the clock never stops, the game is allowed to ebb constantly. And, of course, to flow. Play in the offensive end is constantly developing; like ice hockey or lacrosse, you can watch it open up like a flower, with players cutting for open space and hoping for a lead pass. Or players on the wing faking, juking, and dribbling past defenders in the hope of crossing a pass to an open teammate. Then, when the offensive team loses possession, they retreat on defense, where their opponents try to develop the same kind of opportunities *they* just tried to create. Back and forth, back and forth, for ninety-plus minutes of blissfully continuous action.

Two: it has *creativity*. Definitely a facet of American sports that is disappearing slowly but surely, as high-tech equipment and fitness techniques place the lion's share of attention on power and strength and speed. Thus, in *our* football, we'd much rather see a 60-yard bomb *attempted* than a feathered, finger-tip 4-yard screen pass *completed* any day of the week. Conversely, in football (theirs), creativity and finesse are integral, if not dominating, parts of the game, in the various forms of dribbling, faking, blocking, passing, tackling, heading, crossing, transferring, and so on. There are drives, chips, angles, and bicycle kicks, among many other types of shots. And most of all, except for the hands and arms, nearly every part of the body can be (and is) used! So that a complete player can demonstrate his finesse in dribbling and passing and deception by using his head and neck and chest and waist and hips and groin and thighs and knees and shins and legs and instep and feet and toes. This is not to say that other facets of the game aren't important. To the contrary, it requires extraordinary bursts of speed, power on several kinds of shots, a huge gamut of athletic skills, and stamina unparalleled in the kingdom of sports, to say nothing of tremendous physical and mental toughness. But it's the finesse and creativity that separate it from most other garden-variety games.

Three: it has *true teamwork*. One of the beautiful aspects of any sport, in my mind, is *the assist*. In a sport like football (ours), for instance, many of the offensive plays are built around individual efforts. Despite the blocking of the offensive line and the passing of the quarterback, much of the emphasis is on the individual skills of the running back or the flanker (after the reception). In football (theirs), however, everything is predicated on every player's ability— from the sweeper to the striker—*to set up a teammate for a goal.* Chip the ball over the defense to a teammate's awaiting torso; float it across the field to a teammate's awaiting foot; cross it on a corner kick to a teammate's awaiting head: these are instincts that every footballer— no matter how skilled or brilliant he is individually—develops, always in the interest of the assist (i.e., of *helping* the team to win).

Four: it has *true passion*. Another of the troubles with soccer in the U.S. is that we simply have too many sports to be "passionate" about, which kinda dilutes the passion. Oh, there's baseball, of course, but then there's football (ours) and basketball and tennis and golf and swimming and hockey and snowboarding and in-line skating and. . . . So, under these conditions, how is it possible to develop a national passion about a single sport, much less build a breeding ground for generations to come? How can we feel passionate about a sport that's #1 in popularity in virtually every land on the planet and #7 (and that's being generous) in ours? This general national dilution basically explains why we're so far behind the rest of the world when it comes to football (theirs). And, incidentally, why we placed exactly 32nd out of 32 teams in the most recent World Cup. For the rest of the world, football has deep roots inside the collective consciousness. (Which explains in part why over two billion—yep, that's a *b*!—worldwide watched the World Cup final.) Far from being an elitist sport, it is, rather, the prototypical sport of "the common man." That is, everyone plays it passionately in virtually every nation beyond our borders, from the little toddler in the street to the student in the schoolyard to the old geezer in the vacant lot. Give the average José anything resembling a roundish piece of mutilated leather with a bladder inside—whether he's in Metz or Meknès or Mbuji-Mayi or Mindanao or Managua or Malmö or Mainz or Mazatlán or Manchester or Montevideo or Medina or Madras—and chances are, he'll keep himself occupied by bouncing it between feet and chest and head till, roughly, the cows come home.

What I'm trying to say is that the trouble with soccer in America is, well, America. Starting from *what we call* the game and finishing with *how we see* the game, I'm not sure there's great hope for the future. Hey, don't get me wrong. I love America, partly because of our diversity and our democracy. I love having a huge variety of sports from which to choose, both as spectator and participant. But I don't think we'll ever really have the passion for football that every other country on earth does, simply because we Americans are not born with what geneticists call the NFG (National Football Gene). For your edification, it's that little imperceptible squiggle on the DNA helix that makes a person instinctively avoid touching a ball with his hands upon penalty of death, that makes his feet get frisky and his head get light whenever he is within a centimeter of any ball of essentially round dimensions, and that makes his heart pump like a goddam piston and fill itself to the brim with ecstasy at the very sound of the syllable: GOOOOOOOOOOOOOOOOOOOOOOOOOOOOOOOOOOAL!!!

And *that's* the trouble with soccer.

Where Have You Gone, Sibby Sisti?

Jesus.

It's not just a scary thought. It's a *really* scary thought.

It's been forty-five years since I first cast my eyes upon Sibby Sisti's Bowman baseball card. *Forty-five years.* And since that day, it doesn't take much imagination to figure out how much information has been stored in my three-pounds-or-so of brain matter, with its over ten billion neurons. Nope, it doesn't take a brain surgeon to determine how impossibly over-charged my hippocampus must become from time to time. With a constant stream of information—admittedly mostly useless—piling up against its walls, stuffing into its crevices, cramming into its nooks, sardining into its crannies. Information of every earthly variety, from aardvarks to Zarilla, from anacoluthon to Zernial. Including all manner of tidbits, trivia, details, facts, factoids, information, specifics, data, names, dates, places, titles, theories, theses, hypotheses, thoughts, and opinions in the usual areas of literature, art, music, sports, science, philosophy, psychology, semantics, philology, fashion, travel, theater, and many of the other topics covered in the Sunday *New York Times*.

Now, not only has all that information been depositing itself in a steady stream since the early fifties, but I imagine a great percentage of it has also been forgotten, jettisoned, abandoned, or rejected. Not to mention the fact that our brains supposedly decrease in weight (ergo, in capacity?) by a full ounce every ten years after the age of forty. So the stuff that actually remains after forty-five years should, reasonably, be of such weight and import that it survives the natural selection process and remains intact and untouched by the brain's built-in garbage disposal unit.

On top of all these details, facts, and notions being stored up there, there's also the issue of other stuff, less intellectual than emotive, being stored and generally preoccupying the organ. I'm talking about major cataclysms like Bar Mitzvahs, SATs, weddings, deaths, births, divorces, and having all your earthly baseball cards thrown into the garbage by an unknowing and innocent maternal relative. And all the minor cataclysms too, like wars, pennant races, Joe Cocker concerts, trips (both kinds), unpaid bills, family gatherings, and passing the California driver's license exam.

Yet through it all, through the countless events, morsels of information, and experiences that have occurred and accrued in the past forty-five years and that should have obliterated this puny, insignificant memory from my memory, nothing (I repeat, NOTHING!) has eroded, not even a whit, my recollection of Sibby's $3\frac{1}{2}" \times 2\frac{1}{2}"$ cardboard card.

How can this be?

O.K., let's analyze this thing. We're not even talking superstar here. We're talking about an average, unassuming, unprepossessing, unspectacular, run-of-the-mill journeyman ballplayer from Buffalo who hit exactly .244 lifetime, collected lots of splinters riding the bench throughout much of his thirteen-year career with the now-defunct Boston Braves, and whose real first name—like his arrow-ridden, long-suffering namesake saint—was Sebastian. And who, furthermore, is probably known today by—not counting his immediate family and close friends, of course—perhaps seven other people on the planet. So how do you figure that nearly a half-century after I first collected his card, I still remember him?

What's more bizarre is that I not only remember his card, but I REALLY remember his card! His chiseled face still occasionally haunts my nights, a face that appears to be that of a 60-year-old and that seems to be carved in a painterly, plastic manner out of the cardboard, with the amateurish, chiaroscuro effect of a 1950 photograph. I can still see, in my mind's eye, his fake, static, studied pose: left, gloved hand on left knee, right hand on right knee, as if he were conducting some weird self-examination of his patellas. The pose itself, in fact, suggests the spirit of a troubled poet or even of a self-satisfied orthopedist, but certainly not the youthful, kinetic enthusiasm of a ballplayer. For some reason, I can also remember vividly the fake-looking green outfield grass exactly mirroring the fake-looking green stadium behind him, through which peeked a fake-looking, cloudless sky of robin's-egg blue.

I especially recall a sad, wistful, almost tragic look on Sibby's face (second only in the history of Western civilization to Eve's, as depicted in Masaccio's 1427 *The Expulsion from Paradise*), as if he were freely acknowledging his own mediocrity, as if he were pleading, "Don't collect me. PLEASE, don't collect me!"

Simplify, Simplify

I've always loved this quote of Thoreau's. I guess because it's, well, simple. Two (simple) words, and many of life's difficulties can be made to vanish into thin air. And although I appreciate its wisdom as it relates generally to living, I don't think there are better examples in life of this profound and majestic thought than in the world of sports.

Ever wonder why Nike didn't choose as its themeline: *Just . . . think about it for a while, choose your options, mull it over a bit, explore the various possibilities, add a few refinements, and, uh, . . . do it?*

Now, think for a moment of the thousands and thousands of pitchers ever to throw in the majors. Of all these, the simplest delivery was possessed by a man named Donald James Larsen. Ring a bell? No wind-up. Just came to the stretch, rared back, and threw. Anyway, of all the hundreds of World Series games ever played in the history of major-league baseball, there's been only *one* perfect game.

Guess whose.

Logistically and kinetically, the simplest way to catch a baseball is underhand. In the basket. Of the thousands of outfielders ever to play in the majors, only one (of note) ever caught the ball that way. And he happened to have the greatest-ever relay motion, simply because he saved valuable milliseconds in his wind-up. (His right arm didn't have to be pulled down: it was there already!)

His name? Willie Howard Mays.

The simplest play in football is the power sweep. Just give the pigskin to the fullback, pull your guard and tackle, and let 'er rip. The only truly unstoppable play ever in NFL history?

Does the Taylor-led '66 Packers begin to brush away the cob-webs?

It just seems that whenever we see ostentation and complexity in sports, it doesn't last. What became of the Statue of Liberty? The pick-off play to the second baseman? The four-man weave? Gone, all, the way of the egg cream. Extinct as a stegosaurus! And why? (Hint: *simplify, simplify*.)

Let me put it another way.

You can drive a golf ball one of two ways. You can either bend your knees, keep your feet parallel, align your thumbs, make a "V" at your wrists, tuck in your right elbow, flex your left knee, keep your head down, keep your right elbow close to your body, keep your head down, bring the club back parallel to the ground, leave it there for a beat, explode your hips and your left leg, pronate your right hand at contact, keep your head down, come through with your right knee, take a nice full follow-through, keep your right foot in contact with the ground, and keep your head down.

Or you can—very simply—take a deep breath, swing nice an' easy, and hit the living daylights out of that little white sonuvabitch.

Now It's My Turn

Know how everyone's always spouting off about who's the greatest this and who's the greatest that and the greatest then versus the greatest now? Well, this is, once and for all, where I get to choose my all-time greatests. Players, teams, the works. Of course, it's the prerogative of every sports nut to choose his or her greatests, but *now I get to do mine in print!*

First, a caveat.

I'm not including athletes whom, great as they may have been, I haven't seen perform in person. Thus, many deserving figures—like . Tilden, Perry, Budge, Vines, Kramer, Mallory, Lenglen, Wills, Marble, Jacobs, Sarazen, Jones, Nelson, Hagen, Armour, Thorpe, Mathewson, Young, Johnson, Cobb, Traynor, Speaker, Wagner, Ruth, Gehrig, DiMaggio (the *real* DiMaggio of the forties), Grange, Baugh, Nagurski—are A.W.O.L. So we're basically talking about athletes in the second half of the twentieth century.

Also, a few words concerning criteria. Because the concept "greatest" is so broad and generic, what contributes to such a determination? Certainly, for starters, raw talent. But a lot more than that, surely, or else Lew Hoad, Herb Score, Karl Spooner, Maurice Stokes, Willie Galimore, and Bill Walton—whose careers were all, to some degree, cut short before they could realize their true greatness—might all well be at the top of some of my lists. I don't place too much value on records alone, since they're greatly affected by length of career and quality of opposition. Longevity certainly counts for something (actually, for a *lot*), but it's only part of the picture. Being a "winner"? Surely that counts too, but do we hold that against wonderful "title-less" talents like Ted Williams, Charles Barkley, and Fran Tarkenton? Awards? Consistency? Physical attributes? (The pound-for-pound, "Sugar Ray Robinson" argument: if a guy is 7'2" or built like a Mack truck, is it his fault? Or can someone who gets everything and more out of inferior dimensions be considered "greater"?) Versatility? (Do separate categories have to be made for "specialists" like pitchers, who can't be expected to hit, run, or throw?) Pure dominance? (Wilt, for instance, was clearly the most dominant offensive force ever to play roundball, but was he necessarily the greatest?) All these criteria have to be taken into consideration. But in the final analysis, it's probably other factors that may well tip the scales. Like mental toughness, performance *at crunchtime*, poise, leadership, charisma, and (in team sports) making teammates better.

A word about now versus then. I was fortunate enough to have seen with my own eyes the great players of the fifties, sixties, seventies, and eighties. They tend to get a bit maligned when compared to today's great superstars. In my mind, today's stars are clearly in better shape and more highly motivated (i.e., *financially*). Their competition is keener, since there are more great athletes today than then. And the equipment is certainly much more sophisticated. But if you take all that into consideration, it's my feeling that the players of the "past" are every bit as great as those of today, and in many cases even better.

In any case, to make these judgments, a very fine sense of extrapolation is necessary.

Finally, in the case of a tie, I always invoke the additional criterion of subjectivity. At heart, like most fans and like Johnny Most, I'm basically a "homer." So a brief apology, before starting, for any tendency to lean toward New York teams in general and Willie Mays in particular.

In the end, the question I always pose when making the final selection is "who, if I could choose, would I want serving at match point, or trying for the birdie at the seventy-second hole, or handling the ball or the puck in the final seconds, or at bat/pitching in the last of the ninth with the pennant on the line?"

Ready? Here goes. . . .

GREATEST ALL-AROUND ATHLETE OF ALL TIME

Babe Didrickson Zaharias. Surprise, surprise? So tell me what *guy* has done this: set records in swimming, high jump, skiing, horseback riding, and rifle shooting; struck out Ruth and Gehrig in an exhibition; was an all-American basketball player; was a world-class champion performer in four major sports; won eight events and tied for a ninth (baseball throw, javelin throw, 80-meter hurdles, broad jump, high jump) in the national track and field championships; won two Olympic gold medals (world, U.S. records); was her sex's first fulltime golf professional; won seventeen straight golf titles; won golf's U.S. National Open and the all-American Open after cancer surgery. *I thought so.* Runners-up: four-sporter Jackie Robinson and that greatest-ever lacrosse player and greatest-ever fullback, Jim Brown.

GREATEST DOMINANT ATHLETE, SINGLE SPORT

Wayne Gretzky, hockey. Wilt has the giant's share of the records; Jordan is, well, Jordan. Nicklaus was super over the long haul; Laver had his day in court; Jim Brown and Gale Sayers were unstoppable. But no one comes close to The Great One's dominance. (As Casey would say, you could look it up.)

GREATEST PERFORMERS

Baseball: Willie Mays. Al Hrabosky and Mark Fidrych were great for a short time, and Ozzie was amazing to watch in the field. But for consistent execution, showmanship, and excitement, Willie was who I'd pay to see. Runners-up: Jackie Robinson, Roberto Clemente, Ken Griffey, Jr.
Basketball: Pete Maravich. The greatest, most unpredictable passer/shooter ever. I also loved watching Cousy, Jordan, Barry, Baylor, Monroe, Hawkins, Dr. J., and Magic. But if I had to pay for a front-row seat anywhere, gimme a plane ticket to N'Awlins.
Football: Gale Sayers. Finalists: Jim Brown, Willie Galimore, O.J. Simpson, Hugh McElhenny, Johnny Rodgers, Fran Tarkenton, Barry Sanders.
Hockey: Wayne Gretzky. Runner-up: no one (well, maybe Orr and Lemieux).
Tennis: Ilie Nastase. Finalists: Pancho Gonzalez, Jimmy Connors, John McEnroe. But for shotmaking, arrogance, and showmanship, Ilie was a dilly.
Golf: Chi Chi Rodriguez nips Lee Trevino by a saber.
Boxing: Ali. Runner-up: no one (well, maybe Sugar Ray Leonard).
Soccer: Pelé. Finalists: Eusebio, Chinaglia, Cruyff, Maradona.

GREATEST FRANCHISE OF ALL TIME

Boston Celtics. Runner-up: N.Y. Yankees. The Canadiens are a distant third, followed by the Packers, Dolphins, and Bulls.

GREATEST PLACE TO WATCH A BASEBALL GAME

Boston.

GREATEST PLACE TO HOLD A MARATHON

Boston.

GREATEST PLACE TO MANUFACTURE BAKED BEANS

Boston.

GREATEST COLOR COMMENTARY

Ken Venturi (golf), Mary Carillo (tennis), Tim McCarver (baseball).

BASKETBALL

GREATEST "STARTING EIGHT" (COLLEGE)

Guards: Pete Maravich, Oscar Robertson (alternate: Jerry West).
Forwards: Elgin Baylor, David Thompson (alternate: Tom Gola).
Center: Lew Alcindor (alternate: Bill Walton).

GREATEST "STARTING EIGHT" (PRO)

Guards: Oscar Robertson, Magic Johnson (alternate: Jerry West).
Forwards: Michael Jordan (I know, he's a "guard," but he can play anywhere, and I can't leave out either of my other two guards), Larry Bird (alternate: Elgin Baylor).
Center: Kareem Abdul-Jabbar (alternate: Bill Russell).

GREATEST 21 PROS WHO DIDN'T MAKE MY "STARTING EIGHT"

Guards: Bob Cousy, Rick Barry, Pete Maravich, Earl Monroe, Walt Frazier, George Gervin, Dave Bing, John Stockton.
Forwards: Bob Pettit, Paul Arizin, Dolph Schayes, Elvin Hayes, The Hawk, Dr. J., John Havlicek, Dominique Wilkins, Karl Malone.
Centers: Wilt Chamberlain, Moses Malone, Bill Walton, George Mikan.

GREATEST CAUCASIAN "STARTING EIGHT"

Guards: Jerry West, Bob Cousy (alternate: Pete Maravich).
Forwards: Larry Bird, Bob Pettit (alternate: Dolph Schayes).
Center: Bill Walton (alternate: George Mikan).

GREATEST PLAYER OF ALL TIME

Ninety-nine percent of the pundits will say Jordan because of his incredible *offensive* skills. (Admittedly, he isn't too shabby on defense!) I wouldn't disagree too vehemently, really, but if you're gonna pick an *all-around* greatest player, I have to go against the grain on this one. So I'm calling it a flat-footed three-way tie among the greatest all-around players I ever saw: The Big O, Magic, and Larry. They were all amazingly versatile: they could shoot inside and outside, were big enough to rebound well, played great defense, got lots of steals and assists. Most of all, besides Maravich (and maybe Cousy), they were the best *passers* ever. And (since basketball is a team sport) they did more than anyone ever did (including Jordan) to make their teammates great.

GREATEST CLUTCH PLAYER

Tie: Jerry West, Michael Jordan.

GREATEST LAYUP

Guy Rodgers.

GREATEST JUMP SHOT

Jerry West, Rick Mount.

GREATEST HOOK SHOT

Kareem.

GREATEST HAWAIIAN–BORN CENTER

Red Rocha (Hilo).

GREATEST SINGLE FEAT

Wilt's 28-for-32 foul shots in the 1962 Hershey game against my Knicks. For someone who was a marginal free-throw shooter, this was an *unreal* feat. Runner-up: Wilt's 100 points, same game. Second runner-up: three guys scoring over thirty in a losing cause (Guerin, Naulls, Buckner), same game.

GREATEST UPSET

Texas Western over Kentucky, 1966 NCAA finals.

GREATEST PERSONAL RIVALRY (HIGH SCHOOL)

Connie Hawkins (Boys H.S.) vs. Roger Brown (Wingate).

GREATEST PERSONAL RIVALRY (COLLEGE)

Tom Gola (La Salle) vs. Sihugo Green/Dick Ricketts (Duquesne).

GREATEST PERSONAL RIVALRY (PRO)

Tie: Wilt vs. Russ, Larry vs. Magic.

GREATEST GAME (COLLEGE)

UCLA-Houston, 1968. Runner-up: UNC-Kansas, 1957 NCAA finals.

GREATEST GAME (PRO)

Knicks-Lakers, game 7, 1970 championship.

GREATEST TEAM (COLLEGE)

1967-68 UCLA. Even though they lost a game (that great one to Elvin and Houston), they came back and *demolished* the Cougars in the NCAA semis by thirty-two. A sign of a truly great team to bounce back that spectacularly.

GREATEST TEAM (PRO)

1965 Celtics (the Chicago who?).

GREATEST COACH (COLLEGE)

John Wooden.

GREATEST COACH (PRO)

Red Auerbach.

GREATEST JEWISH PLAYER (PRO)

Dolph Schayes.

GREATEST JEWISH PLAYER (COLLEGE)

Lennie Rosenbluth.

BASEBALL

GREATEST STARTING NINE

Catcher: Yogi Berra. 99% of all pundits would choose Johnny Bench, and (based on numbers) I think they'd have a point. *But:* Yogi could do it all behind the plate, could hit and hit for power, was a *great* clutch hitter (particularly in the Series), and—most tellingly—caught all those Yankee championship teams. And just behind these two, I'd also include Roy Campanella.

1B: Keith Hernandez. With Gil Hodges, the greatest player ever to field the position, plus an amazing clutch hitter. Runner-up: Willie McCovey (amazing on offense, but pales on defense compared to KH). Hodges, White, Cepeda, and Mattingly were great too; and Rod Carew was the best-hitting first-sacker ever, but he wasn't really a pure first-baseman. (P.S. Although Stan Musial spent time at first—especially late in his career—I'm considering him primarily a left-fielder.)

2B: Jackie Robinson. Runner-up: Joe Morgan. The other four *great* ones I've seen are Nellie Fox, Red Schoendienst, Bobby Richardson, and Ryne Sandberg.

SS: Ernie Banks. I also like Aparicio and Reese and Rizzuto and Kuenn and Wills, then Belanger and Trammell and Ozzie.

3B: Mike Schmidt over Brooks Robinson, by a hair. Better power hitter by far, faster, more athletic. But no one could field like Brooks. Honorable Mentions: Eddie Mathews, Ken Boyer, George Brett, Pete Rose (who—yes, Virginia!—should be in the Hall).

LF: Ted Williams and Stan Musial: a flat-footed tie. How could it not be? How could you choose one over the other? Oh, you could argue that Ted hit for a higher average and was a better fielder and had a bit more power. Or, conversely, that Stan had a longer career, thus better overall numbers. If you held a gun to my head, I'd probably go with Stan, mostly for nostalgic reasons (he played in the N.L. and *boy, did he hurt my Jints!*). Runners-up: Frank Robinson (who also played lots of right), Barry Bonds, Carl Yastrzemski, and Lou Brock.

CF: Willie, who else? Mantle is a distant second. (I guess I could also throw in Snider, Ashburn, and Ken Griffey, Jr.)

RF: Roberto Clemente. Even though he was the only batter to strike out four times in an All-Star game (1967), he was the most exciting and versatile right fielder I ever saw. Runner-up: Hank Aaron. Honorable Mentions: Al Kaline, Reggie Jackson.

RHP: Bob Gibson. Best money pitcher I ever saw. Best athlete, best competitor, best curve. Runner-up: Nolan Ryan. Honorable Mentions: Bob Feller, Robin Roberts, Early Wynn, Hoyt Wilhelm, Juan Marichal, Don Drysdale, Tom Seaver, Jim Palmer, Greg Maddux, Roger Clemens.

LHP: Sandy Koufax. Runner-up (by a *hair!*): Spahnie. Show horses: Steve Carlton, Whitey Ford.

GREATEST PLAYER OF ALL TIME

Willie, who else? Runner-up: Jackie Robinson.

GREATEST TEAM EVER

1961 Yankees. Runner-up: 1976 Reds.

GREATEST PITCHING STAFF

1954 Indians (Feller, Lemon, Wynn, Garcia + Narleski, Mossi).

GREATEST OUTFIELD

1954 Giants (Irvin, Mays, Mueller).

GREATEST INFIELD

1976 Reds (Bench, Rose, Concepción, Morgan, Perez).

GREATEST CLUTCH CATCH

Willie's against Vic Wertz, *what else?*

GREATEST CLUTCH HIT

Bobby Thomson's '51 miracle homer in the greatest game ever, *what else?*

GREATEST MOMENT-IN-THE-SUN, CLUTCH PERFORMANCE

Dusty Rhodes' in the '54 Series, *what else?*

GREATEST MANAGER

Casey. Runners-up: Alston, Weaver.

GREATEST COMPETITOR

Jackie Robinson. Runners-up: Sal Maglie, Bob Gibson.

FOOTBALL

GREATEST STARTING ELEVEN (OFFENSE)

Quarterback: John Unitas. At the risk of seeming presumptuous, I'd guess that about 98.6% (that's normal) of today's pundits would pick Joe Montana. As a peace offering, he's my choice as runner-up. It was real close. But if the game were on the line, Unitas is the guy I'd choose. Honorable Mentions: Graham, Van Brocklin, Jurgensen, Starr, Tarkenton, Marino, Elway.

Halfback: Gale Sayers. I *hate* having to choose one. And this is deceptive, since Sayers' career was cut short by injury (a mere five-and-a-half years!), and thus he's absent from the top statistical lists. But if you ever saw him run with the ball, you too would want to give it to him with the game on the line. Close runners-up: O.J. (the most exciting *college* running back I ever saw), Leroy Kelly, Barry Sanders. Honorable Mentions: Walter Payton, Eric Dickerson, Tony Dorsett.

Fullback: Jim Brown: *end of discussion.* Runner-up: Franco Harris.

Tight End: Kellen Winslow. Runner-up: Mike Ditka.

Wide Receivers: Jerry Rice, Steve Largent. Runners-up: Raymond Berry, Charley Taylor, Paul Warfield.

Center: Mike Webster.

Guards: Gene Upshaw, John Hannah.

Tackles: Forrest Gregg, Rosey Brown.

Punter: Ray Guy.

Kicker: Jan Stenerud.

GREATEST STARTING ELEVEN (DEFENSE)

Ends: Deacon Jones, Reggie White.

Tackles: Alan Page, Joe Greene.

Linebackers: Dick Butkus, Jack Lambert, Lawrence Taylor.

Cornerbacks: Mel Blount, Dick "Night Train" Lane/Em Tunnell.

Safeties: Larry Wilson, Ronnie Lott.

Kick Returner: Gale Sayers.

Punt Returner: Mel Grey.

GREATEST COACH

Don Shula. Runner-up:Vince Lombardi.

TENNIS

GREATEST PLAYER (MALE)

Wow, this one's *tough*. The greatest eight I ever saw were Laver, Gonzalez, Hoad, and McEnroe, then Connors, Borg, Rosewall, and Sampras. Laver might have been the purest champion and has amassed the best "record" (e.g., Grand Slams). Pancho was certainly the most "dominant," but that's unfair because the pro-amateur structure then was very different, of course, from today's. Hoad could've been the best ever had he played longer, and Sampras may yet prove himself to be. (N.B.: the business of "most Grand Slam trophies" is a red herring, with all due respect to Emmo. Had Laver and Gonzalez been eligible as pros, each might have won 20 or 30, compared to Emmo's 12!) Rosewall and Connors were (with Gonzalez) by far the most durable greats, McEnroe was the most "talented," and Borg had the perfect temperament and, a *rara avis*, was superb on both grass and clay. But I've finally made my peace, and I'm gonna go with the great Pancho Gonzalez. (Despite the fact that he himself said that Hoad would've probably beaten him if the two were at their best. But Hoad got hurt before he could prove that, and Gonzalez went on for another fifteen years being a great champion.) For a few reasons. First, he was dominant in an absolute sense. Once he turned pro, he took on every amateur champion and *pulverized* them all: Sedgman, Segura, Hoad, Rosewall, Trabert, Laver. Second, he was amazingly durable, beating Laver a year after Rod won the Grand Slam in '69, *when Pancho was 42*! But most of all, it comes down to competitive fury and that criterion I discussed before: at a crucial time in a crucial match, who do I want in there? With probably the most devastating stroke in tennis history (his serve), and a competitive fire second to none, Pancho's my man.

GREATEST PLAYER (FEMALE)

This is really tough too. Most would say that Martina Navratilova was the greatest, based on her athleticism and undeniable record of tournaments won and majors won. I'd say the most graceful I ever saw were Bueno and Goolagong. The most dominant was probably Court. The greatest competitors were Connolly, King, and Evert. Besides Martina, the most athletic were Althea Gibson and Steffi Graf. But here I'm going to be a little inconsistent: for the same reason (shortened career) I almost picked Hoad as the greatest male player but didn't, I'm going with Little Mo Connolly (*barely* nudging out Martina and Steffi). I saw her play in the early fifties, and she was an absolute steamroller. She was reputed to be the fieriest competitor ever in women's tennis, and her record (three straight U.S., three straight Wimbledons, Grand Slam in '53) clearly suggests that, had she continued, she would have amassed a record unmatchable even by the likes of Martina, Chrissie, and Steffi. She was the female version of Pancho, and those are the two I'd want to put up against all comers.

GREATEST MATCH

Borg vs. McEnroe, 1980 Wimbledon finals, was superb. Who can ever forget that amazing 18–16 tie-breaker? But for my money, I'll go with Gonzalez vs. Pasarell, first round of Wimbledon, June 21, 1969. For starters, Pancho was 41 and Charlie was 25! As for the match, all I'll do is present the evidence. On the first day, Pancho lost the first two sets, 22–24, 1–6. The light was failing, both on the court and his career (or so it seemed). Any lesser champion might have thrown in the towel at that point. But the next day, the match was resumed; and

Pancho came back to win, 22–24, 1–6, 16–14, 6–3, 11–9. The record 112 games will never be broken, of course, since tiebreakers were subsequently instituted. The match lasted 5 hours 12 minutes. And to top it off, the aging Pancho was down in the fifth set, 4–5, love–forty, then 5–6, love–forty, and still came back, winning the final eleven points of the match!

GREATEST PERFORMANCE

Chang beats Skoff, 1991 Davis Cup tie. Behind two sets to love, fifth and final match, amidst a hostile Austrian crowd, Michael sucked it up and prevailed.

GREATEST FEAT

Rosewall wins the 1970 U.S. Open, emerging from arguably the greatest field ever. This, *a full fourteen years* after he'd last won the title (destroying Hoad's hopes for a Grand Slam in '56).

GREATEST DISAPPOINTMENT

Four years later, the same Rosewall dropped the final to Connors, 6–1, 6–0, 6–1.

GREATEST WRITER

Over the long haul, it's Bud Collins, of course. But a special mention here to the wonderful scribe and former South African Davis Cupper, Gordon Forbes, whose intelligent and witty writing (*A Handful of Summers, Too Late to Panic*) I greatly admire.

GOLF

GREATEST EVER (MALE)

Jack Nicklaus. *Duh.* (P.S. Although . . . it'd be really amazing to see Nicklaus and Hogan head-to-head. What impels me to make this statement was a factor that Nicklaus never really faced and Hogan faced plenty. A factor that is really key in defining great athletes and that most athletes—great or not—encounter at some point in their careers: hardship. I don't think many athletes could've overcome the physical obstacles that Hogan overcame and perform like he did. Anyway, I'd have loved to see the match-up. And before you start invoking Tiger's name, hold your horses! I'll agree that he's got unbelievable natural talent, but let's not even mention him in the same breath as Hogan and Nicklaus until he's proven his greatness time and time and time again. O.K.?)

GREATEST EVER (FEMALE)

Mickey Wright. Finalists: Babe Zaharias, Kathy Whitworth, Joanne Carner, Nancy Lopez. (P.S. In eight or ten years, talk to me about Annika Sorenstam and Se Ri Pak!)

GREATEST MOMENT

Our amazing, last-day, white-knuckle triumph in the '91 Ryder Cup.

So: there ya have it. My greatests of all time. Oh sure, you don't like some of my choices an' I overlooked this guy an' overrated that guy an' whaddya mean I picked this guy over that guy an' how could I say this guy is better than that guy an' whaddya talkin' about 'cause this guy couldn't hold a candle to that guy an' am I outta my mind sayin' this guy's the best ever of all time???

(God, how I love your passion!)

Golf and Life

If God plays a sport, it must be golf.

For one thing, He'd certainly take up a solo sport, which sort of narrows it down to golf, bowling, figure skating, skiing, and snooker. (For some silly reason, I'm having trouble seeing Him playing the latter four.)

For another, since He moves in mysterious ways, golf must be the sport He must be concentrating on. (A few mysterious thoughts just came to me: who would He have taken lessons from? Who would be his caddie?)

But in the final analysis, golf is, for me, the sport that most clearly represents a microcosm of life itself, an obvious criterion for selection by the Master (after whom, it must be assumed, the great tournament in Augusta was named). It seems to me that although many lessons are to be learned from all sports, golf in particular has the most to teach its passionate practitioners about life and how it should be lived:

HUMILITY. The French philosopher Blaise Pascal, among many others, has pointed out how tiny and insignificant humans are, mere specks in the vastness of the universe. Simple reeds in the morass of the cosmos. And in no single human endeavor do we feel this so excruciatingly as when we shank a shot on the first tee with lots of people watching.

COMPROMISE. The soul of healthy relationships and business deals. So: when you're in the fairway 230 yards from a stream that runs just in front of the green, and you know you can hit a 3-wood exactly 229 yards on the fly, you take out the six-iron, right?

PATIENCE. Have you ever played behind a foursome of older men wearing plaid Bermudas who take all day to putt out?

LIMITS. *Gnothi seauton*, said the Oracle at Delphi. *Know thyself.* Know what you can do and what you can't, says the wisdom of golf. Know that you can't hit the driver on number 5. That traps drive you crazy, so keep it to the right on number 9. And that you're always putting short, so give it a ride. (Or, as the Oracle at Pebble says: *Never up, never in.*)

MODESTY. If you want to show how strong you are, go to an amusement park and ring the bell with the sledgehammer. But strength isn't what it's all about. In life as in golf. Drive for show, putt for dough. Finesse, nuance, touch. True in lots of sports, actually. Bunt a guy over, hit-and-run: you'll score a lot more runs this way than swingin' for the fences. Hey: work on your short game, O.K.?

CHARACTER. You're all alone deep in the woods. No one in the universe is near you to bear witness. Your ball has landed (the odds are 4.7 trillion to one) precisely between a newly-fallen pine cone and a humongous gopher hole. The tree between you and the fairway has only one low-hanging branch, and it just happens to be four inches in front of you and right in your line. And your backswing is hampered by the only red-bellied termite mound in the state of New Jersey. Man, if this doesn't make you a better person. . . .

SACRIFICE. You're back in the woods again (it happens . . .), and you have a choice. Hit your ball through a five-inch opening between two birch trees right onto the green. Or chip out (thus, losing a stroke), and *then* get on the green. P.S. Like Abraham, you don't ask why, you just chip out!

INTEGRITY. What other sport—because it doesn't have umpires or referees—requires you to penalize *yourself*?

. **COURTESY.** And what other sport requires you to make everything nice and neat and clean for *other* people? To keep things tidy (replace divots, rake cleat marks, manicure ball marks)? Maybe it's golf's way of making up for your messy room when you were a kid or leaving popcorn boxes on your seat at the movies. And maybe it really *is* God's game, 'cause you can't get away with that kind of stuff on a golf course!

CONSISTENCY. Ever wonder how those guys on the tour got that good? Besides being well-conditioned, mentally-tough athletes, I think it's mainly because they hit about three *billion* balls a day. I mean, they're like machines when they go out there. *Whack! Whack! Whack!* Every time, the same tempo, the same torque. In golf, as in most sports, you're rewarded for doing things consistently well. And penalized for doing things consistently badly. That goes for the swing and for shot choices as well. As in life: if it ain't broke, don't fix it.

SOBRIETY. Steady as she goes. Keep on the straight and narrow. Sure, you can go crazy once in a while, but as a rule, stay cool, do the right thing, control yourself. Keep your poise in the face of danger. Just like in kindergarten: look to the right, look to the left, then cross. And most of all, stay out of trouble! The rules of life. The rules of golf.

SELF-RELIANCE. Emerson ends his essay on self-reliance as follows: *Nothing can bring you peace but yourself. Nothing can bring you peace but the triumph of principles.* Golf is such a game. Play your game consistently, honestly, and with good cheer, and it doesn't matter what the other guys in your foursome do. Play your *own* ball, worry about your *own* shot, and you'll eventually break 80. (And if not, at least you'll die with a smile on your face.) Not many sports are played with a stationary ball. Why? Because golf is a game of utter self-reliance. Even to the point of requiring *you*, not someone else, to create pace. The only one you can depend on is *you*. I could quote Emerson again, or Thoreau or Boccaccio or Hegel or La Rochefoucauld. But the best quote I can think of is that of the adoring golf fan milliseconds after his pro idol has hit his ball off the first tee: *"You da man!!!!!!!!!!!!!!!!!!"*

RESILIENCE. I can think of no other game in which virtually every single shot you ever hit, every single play you make is completely different from any other one you've ever hit. Except when you tee it up. Why? Because your playing field is God's creation (or man's imitating God). There are no lines you have to keep between, no restrictions (except other people's houses). Because it's played on the ground, the shots you get to take are as varying and as infinite as the undulations of the Earth itself. There is no recipe for each shot, since every shot is a hapax, a one-time deal. Different from the last one and the next one. Ad infinitum. Your shot may be uphill, downhill, sidehill, in mud, dirt, grass, sand, water, or gopher droppings. Against a tree or a bush or a pine cone or a bird's nest. In a trap or a ditch or some idiot's unreplaced divot. And, as in life, you just gotta play the hand you've been dealt. No whining. No crying. Just suck it up, take a deep breath, hit the ball, and go on your merry way.

Boro Park Memoirs

Proust was right, I guess: it's amazing how much we can forget and never fully recuperate. Despite this cruel reality, I still retain—four decades later—vivid memories of my childhood neighborhood, the Boro Park section of Brooklyn during the 1950s.

Then as now, Boro Park had a distinctly Hasidic flavor: her streets were punctuated by the occasional synagogue or *yeshiva* and chatty old men (ancient, they seemed) attired head to foot in black and wearing long, unruly beards. Otherwise, it was still pretty ethnic, mostly Reform Jews and Italians and the occasional Puerto Rican. The nearest Episcopalian could probably be located somewhere across the Pennsylvania border.

I remember the smells of bananas from the peddlers' carts and of sour pickles and herring from the local "appetizer" stores. And the cars parked like so many sardines on the overcrowded streets: not a sleek import in sight, but instead *zaftig*, red-blooded, all-American vehicles whose very names have long since been banished from our collective vocabulary, but that still represent for me a litany of nostalgia: De Sotos, Packards, Hudsons, Studebakers, Nashes, Edsels, Henry Js.

I recall the stores and shops lining Thirteenth Avenue: Linick's Toys (the most important one, where I purchased my Spaldeens), the Schmeelk's and Hessing's luncheonettes, Ebinger's Bakery, Jaynel's Records, Moe Penn Haberdashers (men wore hats in those days), the Skilowitz and Hoffinger's delicatessens, Rothstein's Clothing, the Manny Hanny Bank, The Famous vegetarian restaurant, Miller's Appetizer on the corner of Fiftieth Street (where I purchased a sour pickle straight from the barrel every day on my way home from school). Plus Al del Gaudio's Barber Shop on Forty-ninth, and G & Sons Dept. Store and the Loewe's Boro Park Theater and Monte Greenhut's Mobil Station and El-Gee Electric, all on New Utrecht Avenue.

Ike was President, the War (the Korean one) was over, Uncle Miltie and his Texaco Star Theater were in full bloom on the tube, Elvis wasn't on the scene just yet (but Eddie Fisher, Perry Como, Johnny Ray, Dean Martin, Teresa Brewer, Patti Page, and Ernie Ford were), and you could get the *Times* for just a nickel. Life was pretty innocent then, I suppose.

My brother, my parents, and I lived in a tidy, two-story red brick house on Forty-ninth Street, between Twelfth and Thirteenth Avenues. Dad was a pathologist and conducted business in the front part of the house. I remember the formica-countered laboratory with all its paraphernalia: centrifuge machines, microscopes, slides, test tubes, pipettes, bottles, and Erlenmeyer flasks. I also recall the refrigerator, in whose "Crisper" compartment he used to keep African frogs floating in water, which he used for pregnancy tests. (Actually, for the full and exciting story of the frogs, you can skip to the essay entitled "Siblings at the Pipidrome" after, of course, you finish reading this one.)

But the most vivid memories I have of my childhood were of the games I used to play as a lunatic ballplayer. Most of my friends lived in

Flatbush, so during the week, I was left to my own devices. And these devices, as it turned out, were many and, at times, madly inventive.

It all took place in our driveway. My "home court," if you will. It was, say, fifteen feet wide by about forty feet long. At one end of its length was a two-car garage with an aluminum door; at the other was the street (Forty-ninth). And the two boundaries of its width were the brick side of our house and a long, dark-brown-painted wooden fence. On the other side of the fence were a junk-laden area (the backyard of an appetizer store), accessible by a trap door in the fence, and a tar-covered rooftop area that was behind four or five stores on Thirteenth Avenue. That's it. No trees in the driveway, no dirt, no flora: just cement, brick, aluminum, and wood.

I spent what seemed to be many trillions of hours playing back there, between school and dinner, five days a week. And much of the weekends (when I wasn't visiting my Flatbush friends). And even sometimes after dinner, between dessert and pitch blackness, when, sadly, I would have to come in and do my homework.

It is, thus, nothing less than a miracle—based on my extensive training and dedication and experience—that I didn't eventually become a Major League Baseball Player. Of course, the subsequent intervention of my passion for tennis and the ever-increasing importance of my studies—quick: name a great Jewish shortstop!—had something to do with the thwarting of this (then) very real ambition. Plus, I was probably a lot worse than I *thought* I was (which was, of course, amazing, incredible, unbelievable, perfect, the best in the universe).

The tools of my trade were threefold. First, a floppy black first-sacker's mitt that came to be known as "Ollie." (Ollie was the long-necked, polka-dotted dragon from the popular kids' TV show, "Kukla, Fran, and Ollie." He had two buck teeth, but also a long, floppy mouth that flapped open and shut constantly. Just like my mitt.) Next, I also had with me at all times my trusty Rawlings PM1 mitt, whom I called Hoover (you know . . . the vacuum cleaner . . . sweeps up grounders . . .). And, most important, my Spaldeen. That little pink rubber honey you could squish with your knuckles and when you first bought it, it exuded that wonderful odor of "rubber powder." (More correctly, my *endless succession* of Spaldeens, since I was constantly losing them over the fence or on the roof.)

O.K. Now for the games.

Every game I made up had this in common: they were all contested between the New York Giants and some other N.L. opponent (my favorites were the Dodgers, Phillies, and Cards). They were all based on going through, to varying degrees, the batting orders of both teams in a "recreated" game (harbingers of Les Keiter). And, without exception, the Giants—somehow, miraculously—always won!

First game I remember making up was called "Bottom of the Ninth." It consisted of one simple, repeated act: my throwing the Spaldeen against the garage door into an imaginary box (or, when I had chalk, I'd make four discrete dots, so my Dad wouldn't discover them). That was it. After each delivery, I'd convert myself into an umpire—usually Jocko Conlon or Augie Donatelli—and make a vociferous, gesticulating call. So each batter, without exception, had two options: walk or strike out. Pretty dumb, huh? Well, at the time, it was incredibly exciting. I mean, I really got into it, perfecting my crafty curve and my bullet fastball and all. I would occasionally have inexplicable control problems when the Giants were up (once, I remember walking in eight runs in one inning!). But when the bad guys were up, God, was I great! Virtually unhittable! And calling each pitch was great fun too (in my squeaky yet passionate ten-year-old ump's voice). And seeing myself mow down the heart of the order nearly every time: Furillo, Robinson, Snider, Hodges, Campanella; Ashburn, Ennis, Torgeson, Jones; Slaughter, Musial, Jablonski, Repulski—bring 'em all on, one by one. Bigger they are, harder they fall! Every game took place in the opponent's home park. Every time, of course, it came down to the bottom of the ninth. And every time—the games were typically one-run affairs—Wilhelm or Grissom would come in heroically to snuff out a last-ditch rally.

Then we have "solo stoopball," a variation of the two-man Brooklyn classic. Besides our front stoop, we also had a smallish (three-step) stoop leading up to the back door. The game involved pegging the Spaldeen onto the stoop, whose steps acted as batters. Throw the ball against the steps, catch it. And as usual, I'd go through both orders for nine innings, and whoever won, won (again, somehow it was always the Giants). I especially loved short-hops, but my absolute favorite play was to throw the Spaldeen onto the edge of a step (a "pointer")—creating a vicious, rising liner like the one Bobby hit and Pafko had to watch helplessly as it entered the left-field stands—and then make my incredible and patented "back-back-back-leap-against the-fence-and-just-as-the-ball-is-about-to-disappear-into-the-seats-stretch-my-pipsqueak-body-to-its-absolute-limit-and-snag-it-in-the-webbing-to-the-wild-cheering-approval-of-the-ecstatic-Giants-fans" catch.

Note: After a spirited game of "solo stoopball," I'd usually go in the house for a "seventh-inning snack," which consisted of either two or three packs of Yankee Doodles (amazing quasi-chocolate, creme-filled cupcakes, three to a pack) or three or four individually-wrapped Devil Dogs (same deal, but hot-dog shaped), both compliments of Drake's Bakeries. And all washed down within milliseconds with a glass of good ol' all-American cowjuice.

Now we come to my all-time favorite: "brickball."

To begin with, what I remember most about this game is that I knew every nook, cranny, bump, and irregularity of the brick wall against which I threw my Spaldeen in order to initiate each pitch. Ground rules: throw the ball against the wall so that it bounced back to you. You had TOTAL control over whether it turned out to be a grounder, squibber, bunt, short-hop, liner, Texas Leaguer, pop-up, lazy fly, or towering drive. You just made a split decision prior to each toss, chose your Euclidean angle, and there it was. I usually made the decision based on my incredibly thorough research of each hitter, accrued through many millions of hours studying Bowman and Topps trading cards and box scores, as well as watching every baseball game ever televised in the history of New York. So, for instance, Ashburn would always foul off sixteen or seventeen pitches, then slap a screamer in the hole. Musial would get his token double in the gap. Ennis and Snider would blast towering drives. You get the picture.

Against the Phils, for instance, with Ashburn leading off, I'd peg the ol' Spaldeen on an angle a few times so that it'd go foul according to my own specific, personal ground rules. Then, I'd hit a crack I knew by heart and that I knew would produce a screamer several feet to my left and seemingly out of reach.

But no! (At this point, I put on my Ernie Harwell voice.) *Here comes Hank Thompson from nowhere to snare it on the short-hop . . .* (pause so I can short-hop it in Hoover's awaiting pocket) *. . . he sets . . . he pegs it in the dirt . . .* (now I switch, in the blink of an eye, to Ollie) *. . . but Lockman backhands it just in time to nip the pesky lead-off hitter!!!! . . .* (now I do my "crowd noise") *. . . and the fans go wiiiiiii-iiiiiiiiiiiiiiiiiiiiiiiiiiiiiiiiild!!!!!!!!!!!*

And, as Linda Ellerbee would say, so it goes. Inning after inning. Grounders snared by Williams and Dark, screamers (coming at me at 196 mph from a distance of twelve feet!) intercepted by Antonelli and (against his will) Hamner. Short-hops gobbled up by Lockman. Grounders bobbled by Torgeson. Incredible triple-plays. Drag bunts (remember *them*?). And, best of all, "huggers." These were towering flies that resulted from tossing the ball at a ten-degree angle off the wall, creating a tremendously high arc. After perfecting this play over many thousands of hours, I was almost always able to get my Spaldeen, on its descent, to "hug" the fence just right, so that I need-ed to leap at the last moment to snag it (in the webbing, of course). I usually saved a really great one for the final out (Giants ahead by one, sacks filled with bad guys). For maximum drama, natch.

Often, in the middle of the game, I would get too bold with a "hugger," and the Spaldeen would drop tantalizingly over the fence for a round-tripper. This would happen, oh, six or seven times a game and would necessitate my climbing onto the garage roof via a back-yard stone barbecue, hanging onto a wobbly gutter, and hoisting myself up. Then scaling the roof, up and over to the other side and hopping onto the roof-on-the-other-side-of-the-wooden-fence. The ball might be *somewhere* on that roof. Or it might have bounced to the end and down into the backyard of the appetizer store. Or, worse, it might have ricocheted into a deep well (I called it "The Pit") that I had to climb down into by means of a long, scary, eighteen-foot lad-der and that reminded me of the tank where William Holden had to rescue Lieutenant Dunbar in *Stalag 17* and at the bottom of which were muck and slime and a bunch of still water. In a way, I loved these interruptive scampers because they were adventures, all part of the game, allowing me a momentary break and building up the game's suspense for when I finally wended my way back down to Earth.

These games of "brickball" would last for hours (especially with Ashburn fouling off all those pitches!). And they'd have lasted well into the night were it not for either of two phenomena: Game Called Due To Parking (my father would drive the green Chrysler smack into the middle of the field: *imagine!*) or else Game Postponed Due To Mother Announcing Dinner. And when I finally came in, unwill-ingly and with remorse, I remember always having to employ a bar of *Lava* soap to eradicate my "badges of honor": sweat (from playing), grime (from climbing), grit (from "The Pit"), and dirt (from the appetizer backyard).

And after I washed up, and as I sat down for a lovely meal of salmon croquettes and canned peas or some other indigestible gourmet offering (of course, the Yankee Doodles or Devil Dogs had left little room for *any* kind of further consumption!), and all through dinner, and all through homework, and up until the time—between Ipana and The Sandman—when I finally fell asleep, all I could think of, all I could fill my ten-year-old idiot's brain with, in those wondrous, halcyon, solipsistic days of my adolescence, was how the Jints were gonna eke out yet another glorious victory in the driveway, tomorrow afternoon, starting at three o'clock sharp.

The King of Ibn Gvirol

During the first half-century of my life, the greatest pleasures I ever derived from sports had come from three primary sources: 1. hitting a driver on the screws smack down the middle of an incredibly narrow par-4 fairway, getting a fortuitous bounce on top of that, and landing a scant half-wedge from the apron; 2. executing a perfect lunging touch backhand drop-half-volley off my shoestrings at match-point against an arch rival; 3. going one-on-one with someone at least eight inches taller in my face and burying a jumper (*swish!*) from deep in the corner. But all that changed when I packed my bags for Israel. And when, soon after, on a brilliant spring Mediterranean morning in mid-April 1994, I suddenly became The King of Ibn Gvirol.

I had just arrived from the States, for an eight-month assignment to serve as a consultant at a large ad agency in Tel Aviv. (The Israelis had just instituted commercial television, and I was hired to help them conceive, write, and produce commercials.) I had spent the better part of the first week acclimating: fixing up my apartment on

Pinsker Street, brushing up on my Hebrew (lying fallow since 1957!), preparing lectures and seminars, getting to know agency personnel and procedures, finding a kiosk where I could purchase single-malt Scotch and fresh peanuts, locating the primo falafel and hummus establishments. And, of course, familiarizing myself with the city.

Ah, Tel Aviv!

Whereas Jerusalem is breathtakingly beautiful and ineffably spiritual, Tel Aviv is your basic mishmash. It is at once a spectacular Mediterranean resort with splendid white beaches and deluxe hotels, a bustling commercial center, an ancient site of cultural and historical significance, and a melting pot of many peoples. On a given day, you can wander through the narrow medieval streets of the old city of Jaffa, take a walk up the beach to Picasso's on Hayarkon for a great cup of Turkish coffee and a great view of beach and sea and sky, go up to the open-air market at Nachalat Benyamin, then back to Dizengoff Circle for people-watching and made-as-you-watch strawberry-banana frozen yogurt at Henri's, then up to the art museum for a Dada exhibit, then an early dinner at the Sea Dolphin in the old port (for some wonderful St. Peter's fish or Dennis), and top it all off with a stroll down Sderot Rothschild to a Jackie Mason concert at the Habima theater.

Anyway, once I begin to feel totally comfortable with my new environs, I hunker down to the *real* business at hand: what is there in this town that could satisfy my sporting requirements of fitness and the need for competition? The answers, I soon discover, would far exceed my wildest expectations: as it turns out, Tel Aviv is (pardon the expression) a veritable Mecca for the true sports enthusiast. You want air? There's hang-gliding and aviation. Water? You got windsurfing, swimming, snorkeling, scuba diving, waterskiing, fishing, boating. Land? The sports of preference (in fact, they're crazy about them) are soccer (er, football), basketball, and tennis. The former two are practiced all over the city, particularly in the sprawling *Sportek* complex in Yarkon Park. As for tennis, I ended up playing in no fewer than nine wonderful clubs or tennis complexes, the granddaddy of which is *hamercatz letennis beyisrael* (The Israel Tennis Center) in Ramat Hasharon, where I coached a bit, played, and enjoyed watching the young Israeli *wunderkinden* develop under the expert tutelage of Ronnie Sender, Ian Fromin, and their talented staff of teaching pros.

But there's one final sport I've been saving for last. It's one I've been enjoying for about seven years now, and to which, I quickly discover, Tel Aviv beautifully (even uniquely) lends itself.

Rollerblading.

Tel Aviv is ideally suited for blading lunatics for two reasons. First, there's a wonderful oval track in the *Sportek* complex: it's huge (it takes about 28 seconds to complete a lap if you're *really* jamming), made of smooth green concrete, and surrounded by an iron fence, all in a serene, isolated setting. And the streets of the city are, for the most part, well paved, extremely smooth and dry (a *sine qua non* for effective blading), and exceedingly flat.

At the end of my first week, I begin a routine that I would continue to follow for the entire eight months, never missing a single day (except when I was traveling). I'd get up at seven, make coffee, put on my gear, and be out of the apartment by 7:30. The route I map out is simple: down Pinsker, bear left onto Dizengoff, turn right onto Ben Gurion, left onto Ibn Gvirol, then straight up Ibn Gvirol, uphill over the bridge, then bear right into the *Sportek*. Once there, I'd blade around the oval track for an hour (about 100 laps), then return home, retracing my steps.

The oval is lots of fun, auto-competitive (I try to see how many laps I can do in an hour), and terrific exercise. But it is the experience of blading through the streets that proves not only invigorating, but absolutely memorable to boot.

Especially Ibn Gvirol.

At that time, I was one of the very few practitioners of the sport in Tel Aviv (i.e., in Israel). There were, of course, a select number of enthusiasts who bladed in the *Sportek*. (Why else would the Israelis have spent so many shekels to build such an impressive track?) But I rarely encounter any other bladers in the streets. And you had only to blade once through the streets (especially Ibn Gvirol) to understand why.

Let's put it this way: imagine rollerskating down the main drag in Pamplona during the "running" season, but instead of crazed bulls, you have crazed drivers in two-ton metal vehicles to deal with.

Now, I've seen traffic all over the world. From the chaotic pattern circling the Arc de Triomphe in Paris to the Teutonic demons on the Autobahn to the possessed Italians to New York cabbies to Boston drivers (who apparently still haven't discovered that cars come equipped with these things called directional signals). But Israeli drivers—they take the cake.

Apparently, because of the extreme year-round tropical clime and the fact that there's always tension in the air (imminent wars and the like), drivers in Tel Aviv vent all their pent-up hostilities when they climb behind the wheels of their cars. Remember those "bumper cars" in the amusement park? Well, that's exactly what it's like: if you're in your car driving down the street, it's an extremely hazardous, harrowing enterprise just getting to your destination intact. Now imagine *blading* down the street, slaloming around cars, a potential victim at every turn. On top of it all, Israeli drivers are pretty possessive about their own space. They see pedestrians as obstacles; so when they see a crazy, cockamamey blader, in full regalia (funky wraparound sunglasses, neon-green kneepads, purple handguards, purple shorts and matching Williams College T-shirt), well, they see red. In fact, even if you keep to the extreme right of the street, apparently out of harm's way, they frequently veer out of their way to within millimeters of your left foot to take an affectionate "swipe." Just their charming way of saying, "Hi there, I'm hot and sweaty and on the lookout for Iraqi fighter jets and my eight-inch penis is in no mood to deal with some idiot on weird skates dressed like he's from outer space and sharing the same road, so have an exceedingly pleasant day and here's to your continued health and safety!"

At first, it's pretty scary negotiating this whole scene. But by degrees, I become slightly less apprehensive, then sort of comfortable, then pretty confident, then downright defiant. Who the hell are *they* to be so nasty? What right do they have to resent my very existence? And soon, the ride up Ibn Gvirol evolves from being an ordeal to becoming a Goddam Mission.

Every morning, at the very moment I turn left onto Ibn Gvirol and start to hit traffic, in addition to getting exercise and enjoying the sport, I receive immense doses of joy in showing 'em who's boss. They'd sideswipe me? I'd wait for 'em to stop at a light and give 'em a fist thump to the hood. They'd fire obscenities at me? I'd give 'em right back, in either language (actually, a wonderful way to pick up some colorful expressions in a foreign tongue). They'd give me the finger? Right back at you, Moishe. Until, at one point, I think the motorists who encounter me on a regular basis suddenly develop a certain respect for my new-found aggressivity and disdain. A maniac after their own heart, I suppose. In a funny way, Ibn Gvirol has become my *own* turf; and, since I have the advantages of compactness and maneuverability over them, I actually hold a decided advantage! Now it is *they* who'd have to give way, to accede, to bow down, if you will. And the attendant feeling I experience, as I whiz down the avenue in my own private space, is nothing short of downright uplifting.

And before I know it, this new status becomes somehow apparent not only to drivers, but to pedestrians as well. What was formerly an annoyance and a strange interloper is now being perceived by many as an appealing novelty, a desirable aberration, a phenomenon to be emulated, A Force To Be Reckoned With! Total strangers in both the driver's and passenger's seats would wave to me and shout affectionate *manishmas*, *mashlomchas*, and *shaloms*. Pedestrians and café habitués would greet me, as if I were passing by in the final stage of the Tour de France or the Boston Marathon. And, on more than one occasion, a friendly soul would even bow down and swing his arm down in a flourish, as one would do to allow a royal figure to pass, in abject (albeit mock) adoration.

Yes: it is now an accepted, unalterable fact, and one of the great sporting moments of my life: I have indeed become The King of Ibn Gvirol!

Many months after I return to the States, I receive a letter from Leo and Margaret Schwartz, two of the loveliest people on the face of the earth and dear, longtime friends (they live in Ramat Gan). During the course of the missive, they inform me that rollerblading has become a widespread pastime in Tel Aviv since my departure. And as I finish the letter, I am left with the perhaps delusionary feeling that my reign as King has in fact spawned an entire population of imitators, emulators, and pretenders. That, in their minds, I am now seen as a forerunner, a pioneer, a Patriarch. And, my addled thinking continues, they've even constructed a statue in my likeness, draped in my crazy blading outfit, at the corner of Ibn Gvirol and Ben Gurion, for all to revere and remember. And—why not?—maybe they've even placed me in the august company of Theodor Herzl, Chaim Weizman, Meir Dizengoff, and David Ben Gurion by renaming Ibn Gvirol *itself* after me?

So, if you ever end up in Tel Aviv and happen to be driving (or rollerblading) east on Ben Gurion Boulevard, track me down, drop me a line, and let me know if it eventually intersects with Bob Mitchell Avenue.

It'd really make my day.

Desire under the Pines

Inside every athlete, there's something deep down in the viscera that is responsible for the will to compete, to excel, to get the most out of oneself. But what is the genesis of this feeling? The answer may vary according to the individual, ranging from upbringing to environment to early models to some genetic quirk.

In my case, it owes a lot to watching Freddie Eppsteiner.

Freddie was a campmate at Camp Takajo in Naples, Maine, where, between 1953 and 1960, I spent eight of the most glorious summers of my life. Freddie was a cheery, likable, nice kid who had one feature that separated him from the other 249 campers.

Freddie had had polio and wore cumbersome braces on both legs.

The first time I played in a baseball game with Freddie, I guess my reaction was the same as any other spoiled, unthinking ten-year-old's. *How sad. What a shame. What a pity. Thank God it's not me.* As I watched Freddie clank his way down to first base, my own feelings of insulation and self-importance would naturally surface. Feelings that were somewhat less than compassionate, bordering on pity.

Freddie would almost never get on. Or, once in a blue moon, he'd hit a slow roller to the left side that the third-sacker would throw wildly, *way* over the first-baseman's head, deep into the woods, and behind some blackberry bush. By the time it was retrieved and finally thrown back to the bag, he'd barely beat it out by a whisker, causing the guilt-ridden fielder to hang his head in shame.

And shame is what I, idiot ten-year-old that I was, must've felt until I realized the amazing heroism of this kid. *Imagine.* He was thrust into a situation where he was surrounded by a group of basically decent athletes, some even extremely gifted. And all "normal." But what was amazing was his good cheer. Well aware of the "unlevel" playing field caused by his handicap, he would limp his way to first base time after time, hunching up his shoulders to give himself some inertia (and perhaps to absorb God knows what pain), braces clanging, head jerking back, arms flailing. *And a smile on his face!*

In point of fact, I don't ever remember seeing him without that hopeful, cheery smile. *Ever.* And to this day, my visual image of Freddie— smiling all the way down the first-base path on his way to an inexorable 1–3, 2–3, 6–3, 5–3, 4–3, or 3 unassisted—remains as clear and compelling as ever.

Truth is, even though I never told him (I wish I had) and even though he never knew it (I wish he had), I came to admire and respect Freddie in a special way I never felt with any other athlete before, during, or since. And what I most respected, in those innocent days under the sweet-smelling Maine pines, was his *desire.* More than anyone else, Freddie *wanted to play the game.* Not to succeed, as we "others" did, pushed by some Western, goal-oriented, "achievement" ethic. Not to please someone else (parents? counselors? older brothers?). But simply to play, to participate, *to be there.*

Freddie's desire to play was never more evident (I find it some-what frightening that I still remember the incident vividly to this day) than in the 1956 version of the Annual Camp Takajo Soda Pop Baseball Game, or ACTSPBG.

(This is going to take a little explaining.)

In those days of relative non-permissiveness, discipline, and priva-tion, the summer-camp environment was in fact closer to that of a boot camp. There were strict rules of conduct, one of which was that under absolutely no circumstances was any candy or soda pop allowed on the premises. Except, of course, for the weekly "candy sale," at which time you were allowed to buy one single solitary piece of candy. (Note: the most popular candy in those days were Charleston Chew, Bonomo's Turkish Taffy, Clark Bar, and—a distant fourth—Zagnut.) Even during Visiting Day, parents were told in no uncertain terms that candy and soda pop were strictly forbidden as "bunk gifts." (Of course, in their parental zeal, they rarely listened, and transgression of this particular ruling was rampant.)

Oh. The ACTSPBG. . . .

Anyway, it was a game to which every camper looked forward eagerly. Which was strange, because the camp was so competitive (intercamp games in baseball, basketball, and tennis, plus tournaments in all three sports), and other "special" events, to be scheduled, had to be squeezed in between events of greater competitive substance.

Here's how it went. There were actually two games, one for the junior camp, one for the senior camp. In each game, you got up (against "good control" counselor pitching, so walks and boredom weren't factors) and took your cuts. In the first- and third-base coaching boxes were positioned waiters from the mess hall (remem-ber that "boot camp" thing), in whose strong arms were nestled serv-ing trays filled with cups and a number of bottles of assorted sparkling beverages: Coke, Nedick's Orange, Hires Root Beer.

Why the game was so popular had everything to do with the system of reward in this environment of privation: if you got a single, they gave you a cup of soda; a double, you got two cups; a triple, three; and a homer would allow you to gulp down an entire bottle! Of course, conversely, an out would reward you with absolutely zippo. Talk about motivation!

Naturally, every camper was dying to get *at least* one hit and, deep down, dreamed privately of hitting four homers. I forget how I performed under these pressure-packed conditions. I think I got my share of hits, including a few triples. I certainly remember a couple of liners where I got robbed, not so much of an extra-base hit, but of several cups of ambrosia: a screamer down the third-base line that Lew Burke snared with his eyes closed and a frozen rope in the hole that (ironically) Tiger Goldberg pulled out of his friggin' rectum to rob me of Lord knows how many bases.

But the memory of these games that's most vivid is the time Freddie came up and, to the surprise of virtually everyone on the field (and off: word travels fast in camp), got hold of a fat one and just *creamed* it. I mean, he got every inch of it, the way I'd never seen him get hold of one during "non-soda pop" skirmishes. And, smile on his face as always, he hobbled off to first (to which base he was totally unaccustomed) and, realizing the ball was still traveling down the rocky road beyond left field and past two bunks (Illinois and Iroquois), stopped briefly in shock before beginning to make his way to second. *Second!* Freddie's even contemplating reaching second base was like America's contemplating landing on the moon in the early fifties. But reach it he did, in plenty of time to beat the throw, which at long last made its way, via two or three relay men, to second base. I think for a split instant Freddie actually contemplated trying for third but, appreciating the already-prodigious feat of doubling and not wanting to tarnish its memory, thought better of it and stayed frozen to the bag. At this point, it was like a movie: as if in slow motion, campers began, one by one, to applaud, until *everyone* was paying tribute to Freddie's feat (and feet). Then, as the applause reached a fever pitch, the waiter (it was Arnie Abrams, as I recall, who, incredibly, is *still* at Takajo over forty years later!) trotted out to give him his just desserts (the two cups of pop). Freddie had done the impossible. And in the ACTSPBG, no less!

Since then, I think I've especially appreciated several aspects of athletic competition (and life) more than I ever would have had I not seen Freddie Eppsteiner perform on a baseball diamond. Never give up. Be true to your inner voice through all the ups and downs that might befall you. Pressure? *What pressure?* And, finally, as you run down that first-base line of life, keep smiling. Oh, above all, keep smiling.

The Virtues of Pennyball

Any athlete worth his or her salt can talk to you at great length about the virtues of most sporting endeavors. Baseball, basketball, football, soccer, and hockey, they will assert, can teach us the values of unselfishness, discipline, and team play. Golf, tennis, bowling, and billiards, they will continue, can teach us the values of focus, preparation, and execution under extreme pressure. Gymnastics, figure skating, skiing, swimming, and track and field, they will conclude, can teach us the values of conditioning, flexibility, and poise. But who *ever* talks about the virtues of pennyball, huh? It is the purpose of the diatribe that follows to correct this woeful gap in the history of human sporting expression.

For those of you who have never heard of this important but virtually forgotten sport, pennyball was purportedly conceived in Brooklyn in the late 1500s. It is an ancient pastime greatly revered even today by a loyal, albeit regrettably small, group of practitioners.

Because of its beauty and simplicity, it is the ultimate Zen sport. All you need is a penny and a ball. That's it. The penny can be from any year whatsoever and may even be an Indian-Head. The sport is also flexible and forgiving, since in a pinch, if a penny isn't available, a dime will suffice. Further, although a pink Spaldeen (preferably, a "first") is recommended, substitutes are deemed acceptable, including other brands of rubber balls and tennis balls of any year, make, or model. And, to top it off, it is wonderfully universal, in the sense that you can play it virtually anywhere in the world where there are sidewalks with cracks.

Here's how it works. You and your opponent choose any three consecutive cracks in a sidewalk. You station yourself behind one of the outer cracks, your opponent stations himself behind the other outer crack, and the penny is placed right in the middle of the center crack. Then, you take turns tossing the ball toward the penny in an effort to hit it (the toss must be overhand). You get one point every time you hit the penny. First to an agreed-upon total (usually ten or twenty-five) wins. That's *it*!

Oh. There are, as in any competitive sport, nuances. When you hit the penny, as I've stated, you get a point. But, as in life, there are two sides to this coin. Because at the same time as you're rewarded for the "hit," you're also penalized, since the penny generally will move *toward* your opponent, making his subsequent turns easier (because now he's closer to the penny) and yours more difficult (you're farther from it). Conversely, if he hits the penny, his next turn(s) will be more difficult, and yours easier. Where the nuances come in: there are ways to avoid the "penalty" part if you're very skilled and a little lucky. You can use backspin on your toss so that, if it hits the penny in exactly the right spot, it'll cause the penny to move backwards, *towards* you! Resulting in your being doubly rewarded: you get the point, and your next turn(s) will be easier, not more difficult.

But what are the lasting values we can take away from this seemingly esoteric and jejune sporting endeavor?

1. *Discipline.* It takes lots of self-control and focus to block out everything in the universe except for that ball and that penny. 2. *Variety.*

In pennyball, as opposed to some other sports, you can't be a one-trick pony. Nope, you've got to become a master of spins, knowing when to throw flat, when to put backspin or sidespin, when to hit the penny in the solar plexus and when to give it a glancing blow in the ribs. 3. *It's all in the wrist.* Well, it is! 4. *Resilience.* The coin is, of course, the supreme metaphor for life's vicissitudes ("flip of the coin," "make a wish," "bounce of the coin," "other side of the coin". . .). And pennyball requires of its practitioners the rare ability to adapt to ever-changing circumstances, conditions, and distances and to alter one's perspective, approach, and execution accordingly. 5. *Poise.* When you're constantly being confronted with changing conditions and the to-and-fro of the fickle penny, you've got to maintain your equanimity. Otherwise, your nerves are likely to jangle, your brow will become dotted with beads of sweat, and your hands will quake and tremble. Every toss—and *yours* comes at an average rate of one every 1.7 seconds—puts your poise and nerves to the supreme test: you are *constantly* a combination of the short reliever in the bottom of the ninth, the guy at the free-throw line with two seconds left and his team behind by two, the place-kicker trying a field goal with no time left and his team behind by two, the center trying a penalty shot at 19:59 of the third in an attempt to send the game into OT, the golfer trying to hole a four-footer on the seventy-second hole to tie for the lead, the server at 5–6 in the tie-breaker who needs to hold in order to force further play.

And if anyone who lacks the knowledge of Brooklynese history and culture should dare tell you otherwise, or *for one second* hint that pennyball is a sissy sport that doesn't require any of the classic athletic attributes such as endurance, speed, power, finesse, and agility, well, you can just tell him two things, and you can say you heard them from me.

You can just tell him *up your nose with a rubber hose,* and *you're so funny I forgot to laugh.*

Dewey Defeats Truman!

It's October 3, 1951, it's the bottom of the ninth of the final game of the pennant playoff series, and the Giants are trailing the Dodgers by three runs in the most dramatic, pressure-filled game in the history of baseball. After coming from thirteen-and-a-half games behind in mid-August, their luck has finally run out, and the prospect of winning would be, at best, an incredibly long shot. And, wouldn't you just know it, the expected is just what happened. A brave and untouchable Branca strikes out Dark, Mueller, and Irvin in succession, and Dem Bums leave the field mobbing Branca, their hero, and begin to prepare mentally for the Series with the hated Yanks.

It's 1955, it's the final round of the U.S. Open, and the upstart and unknown driving-range pro, Jack Fleck, will obviously fold down the stretch in his attempt to beat the unflappable golfing machine known around the universe as Ben Hogan. And so he does: like a concertina, Fleck folds, unsurprisingly, and Hogan waltzes to yet another glorious, predictable major.

It's 1964, and there's a cocky, inexperienced heavyweight mouthing off at the world that he can whoop the imposing, intimidating, unbeatable Leviathan by the name of Sonny Liston. Fat chance. And in fact, Sonny indeed decks the cocky Clay at 1:12 of the very first round.

It's 1966, and the heavily-favored Kentucky basketball five led by Pat Riley and Louis Dampier are taking on the no-name Texas Western squad in the NCAA finals. Texas *Who*? The Wildcats win, naturally. In a walk. I mean, who are these pretenders, anyway?

It's 1969, and the upstart Jets are in the Super Bowl. Playing against—gulp!—the powerful, unbeatable Colts, who have the greatest QB ever and the greatest back-up QB ever. And the Jets? Another braggart (like Clay) calling signals and a pretty good all-around squad. But beat *Baltimore*? You're just whistlin' in the wind! And whaddya think happens? Yep: Colts 35, Jets 0.

It's still '69, and now it's October, and another team from Gotham is playing for all the marbles. The Mets beat the *other* team from Baltimore? G'wan. Sure, they got a pretty good pitching staff, but look at the O's on the mound! And besides having to match up with Cuellar, McNally, and Palmer, the Metsies are Little Leaguers compared to the Birds' firepower at the plate. Well, sir, you guessed it: Birds sweep. So what else is new?

It's 1973, and 69-year-old Bobby Riggs is trying his luck against one of the great women's tennis players of all time. A woman who was *named* after the playing field, for chrissake! Margaret *Court*! And Riggs, he was great in his time. I mean *great*. But now? Gimme a break. He waddles, has no speed, and is nothing but a bag of aging wind. Margaret, on the other hand, is young, strong, powerful, gifted, and cool as a cucumber. Riggs win? Don't make me laugh. Final score: Court 6–0, 2–0, ret.

It's 1980, and our young, idealistic, pie-in-the-sky Olympic hockey team's taking on the Russian six that's the equivalent of the Celts, Yanks, and Packers rolled into one. Well, at least we've got a shot. *Right.* The morning line has Russia by eight goals, and, boy, they were right on the money.

It's 1998, and a low-scoring soccer team from hosting France— which had eked out a win over Italy by penalty kicks and then a one-goal squeaker over surprising Croatia—is pitted in the World Cup finals against the exciting, star-studded, explosive juggernaut that is Brazil. No contest. Bet the ranch on the yellow-green-and-blue boys from the land of samba. And guess what. You kept the ranch and won your bet: your Portuguese-speaking hotshots went crazy and creamed their Gallic opponents, 12–nil!

My (sarcastic) point? Simple: what makes sports wonderful, excit- ing, passionate, and magical isn't so much the skill level, the perfor- mance per se, or the spectacle itself. Oh, all these are great, don't get me wrong. But what's really special about sports is what it has in com- mon with life: it's totally, deliciously *unpredictable.* What you think can never happen often does; what you think must surely happen often doesn't. Ever stare at the NCAA draw and pencil in your projected winners, only to find some unknown team from northeastern Oklahoma upsetting some Big-Ten powerhouse in the first round? Or did you lay a grand on Iron Mike when he met James "Buster" (who-*he?*) Douglas? O.K.: Ray Floyd's sitting in the clubhouse with the lead during the final round of the PGA, and Couples, Faldo, Woosnam, and Price are charging down the homestretch. So, how many people out of a hundred can pick the eventual winner? In my opinion, the 1970 U.S. Tennis Open was comprised of the strongest field in its history: Laver, Roche, Newcombe, Nastase, Smith, Ashe, Richey, Okker, and the list goes on and on. So what happens? Does Laver or Roche or Newcombe win? Nope: Ralston upsets Laver (who'd won the Slam the year before), and out of the eminent pack emerges . . . Ken

Rosewall, *age 36*, who'd previously won the event a full fourteen years prior, preventing Lew Hoad from winning the Slam.

The powerful visual images we retain from sports' greatest moments are, to a large degree, those of unexpected, unpredictable moments frozen in time: Bill Buckner's wide-open legs (and the wide-open mouths of Mets fans) in the '86 Series; Dan Jansen smashing disconsolately (and astonishingly) into the padded Olympic boards; Jim Valvano's wild rush onto the court following the Wolfpack's improbable upset of Houston; the wild ending, complete with trampling of college band, following the ridiculous gridiron surprise of Stanford by Cal; Michael Chang's dazed body collapsing onto the Parisian clay after his unexpected defeat of Lendl; and, of course, the aforementioned (reverse) images of a hyperkinetic Thomson, a disbelieving Fleck, a prostrate Liston, a dazed Rupp, a gloating Namath, a mound of jubilant Mets, a smug Riggs, a benumbed U.S. Olympic hockey squad, and a gleeful band of Francophonic footballers.

And if you still cling to the fantasy that you should always bet on the favorite, just go to any reputable volume on American History and see what President Dewey had to say regarding the matter.

White Wigwams, Bent Hanger

Oh sure, the wheel was good. And the electric light bulb, the airplane, and the computer weren't too shabby either, as far as inventions go. But for pure creativity, I don't think anything will ever approach the brilliance of what I'm about to describe.

It all happened during a sleep-over date at the home of Jimmy Blumstein, a high school classmate and fellow thirteen-year-old sports nut. (Today he's—*oy!*—an eminent law professor at Vanderbilt.) On East 24th between N and O in Flatbush. It was a Saturday evening in early April of 1958, as I recall. (To tell the truth, this is a bit of scriptural prevarication: I can't recall what day of the week it was that I had my last haircut, much less an event that occurred over forty years ago!)

Anyway, we had spent the entire day competing in every imaginable game that little human beings could play on the streets and sidewalks of Brooklyn: basketball in the backyard (one-on-one, horse, around-the-world), stickball, stoopball, boxball, wallball, pennyball.

Then inside for some board games (Parcheesi, Rich Uncle, Clue, Monopoly, Boom or Bust) and basement hockey and fifty games of ping-pong (twenty-one wins) and baseball-card flipping games ("heads or tails," "leaners"). Then outside again for punchball, sewer hockey, football-throwing-for-accuracy-and-distance, fungo.

Now, when I say competing, I mean *competing*. Each event, no matter how trivial, was a serious life-and-death matter. Oh, we had fun, but there was always so much at stake, and our common desire to battle to the death was somehow always paramount. I think most of the fierceness and fury of our competitions resulted from the fires that burned within each of us, the common desire to compete (and to win), as well as that stupid macho pride thing. But part of the deal, I think, was sociological: in the fifties, each facet of life seemed to present itself strangely as a one-on-one, head-to-head, do-or-die competition. Today, everything is multifaceted, polyvalent, complex, disparate. Then, there always seemed to be just two of each: Robinson vs. Basilio, Pep vs. Saddler, Giants vs. Dodgers, Browns vs. Lions, Brown vs. Huff, Willie vs. Duke, Hogan vs. Snead. But not only in sports: it was also Colgate vs. Ipana, Fab vs. Tide, Hershey's vs. O'Henry's, Corn Flakes vs. Rice Krispies, Macy's vs. Gimbel's, Swayze vs. Murrow, Berle vs. Benny, Perry vs. Eddie, Marilyn vs. Jane, Roy vs. Gene, Murray the K vs. Cousin Brucie.

As darkness fell, we were called in for dinner and grudgingly acquiesced. As I recall, we couldn't have been very hungry, since we had been coming in all day long for frequent snacks (to refuel our growing adolescent bodies), which consisted of Devil Dogs, Yankee Doodles, and our favorite drink, a soda-and-milk concoction. (My favorite soda to include in the murky mixture was Hoffman's cream soda, with Cott's a close second; Jimmy's was Nedick's orange drink.) What I also recall was the thick carapace of dirt, muck, sweat, and grime that oozed off our skin and down into the sink as we washed up for dinner. In those days (way before two-income families), there existed two phenomena in households that are, for the most part, long gone today: families ate together, and there were rules. One of the basic rules of etiquette was that, for whatever reason, everyone who sat down to dinner should be spotlessly clean. So there we were, Jimmy and I, sadly removing our badges of honor as the layers of dirt spiraled down the drain. (A technological postscript: at about this time, some R&D genius—undoubtedly a parent himself—had invented a product called *Lava* soap to deal with this sort of profound dirtiness. It was made up of a combination of tallow and steel wool that could've removed the paint job off a '56 Studebaker.)

After a scrumptious meal of lima-bean-tasting vegetables and some meat-loaf thing (apologies to Mrs. Blumstein, who was probably a superb cook: to me, *every* dinner tasted like lima-bean-tasting vegetables and some meat-loaf thing), Jimmy and I repaired to his room, played twenty or thirty more board games, watched some TV, went to the basement and played ten more games of ping-pong, returned to his room for some more TV (raucous wrestling: we rooted against Mr. Moto), and then—after Mr. Blumstein intruded and asked us ever-so-politely to keep it down to a dull roar—settled down to quiet conversation. *Quiet conversation?* Now, anyone who has ever had an adolescent, pre-pubescent son who's athletically inclined and thus has a metabolism of a zillion knows that eventually, quiet conversation will give way inexorably to something a great deal more active. And so it did. Impelled by the need to rev up our bodies once again and re-assume the heartbeats of hummingbirds, we set our minds to concocting a game that could be played in a room, could continue indefinitely, was intensely competitive, and was some (re)incarnation of a major sport. After searching our brains and his room for an hour or so, we were about to give up in frustration when it suddenly, miraculously occurred to us.

HANGERBALL!!!!!!!!!!

The idea for the game was devilishly, maniacally simple. First you take one of those wire coathangers you get from the cleaner's. Then you bend it into a circle (actually, a polyhedron of some kind, due to its rigidity). And that's your basket! We figured that an acceptable height for the basket would be the top of the door (plus the transom was the only place we could think to hang the hanger from), so we wedged it between door and transom, and there it hung majestically. We experimented with a number of ball ideas—whiffle ball, Spaldeen, tennis ball, ping-pong ball(!)—all of which were vetoed instantly by Jimmy's Dad, who, judging that the noise made by our dribbling was unacceptable, kept intruding to affirm his official umpire's opinion. Finally, after countless failed experiments at "ball muting," we discovered the perfect silent ball: an old, wrinkled pair of white Wigwam socks (folded up the way you fold them up when they come out of the dryer). How ironic: the perfect ball didn't even bounce! (We ultimately discovered that an orthodox ball just would-n't hack it sound-wise, so we decided to improvise for the express purpose of going bounceless.)

After numerous painstaking refinements, the official rules were passed into law. No dribbling, but you could fake-dribble, bobbing the pair of socks up and down as you grasped it in your palm, which it obviously never left. Walking was allowed, of course, as were dou-ble-dribbles. So that, unencumbered by the demands of ball-han-dling, the player in possession only had to be concerned with his inexorable movement toward the basket and positioning himself for the shot. We also decided, after some trial and error, that there should be no fouls called. Otherwise, the game would be spent entirely at the foul line, since (often vicious) fouling was the only way to dis-courage a continuous offensive barrage. Oh: buckets were two points.

Now, you gotta get the picture visually. There we were, one crazy lunatic wildly toting this sock-ball-thing in his sweaty little palm, bouncing up and down to the soundless rhythm of his fake-dribble, menacing his stealthy way toward a floating ersatz coathanger-basket squeezed into the door opening, while the other is bumping, shoving, pushing him away from his intended destination with the fury of a Sam Huff-Chuck Bednarik-Alex Karras amalgam, shadowing, shadowing, all over him like a rash. And all of this adolescent lunacy is transpiring in dogged, earnest silence, with only the grunts and muffled ouches of battle intruding themselves, as if apologetically, into the intense, excruciating noiselessness.

With all the fouling and pushing and shoving, you'd think it'd be a low-scoring, unexciting defensive affair. Boy, would you be wrong! You see, in those days, scoring (for the pros as well as us amateurs) was (slightly) less a matter of brute force than of finesse and tactical maneuvering. So it was all a matter of fakes. You'd go left, then right, then free yourself for a Guy Rodgers scoop lay-up. Or you'd go right, then left, then find room for an unblockable hook (banked, naturally) from Houbregs or Foust or Johnston or Kerr. Or you'd fake in toward the basket, then back up for a Gola push. Or you'd fake, like Sweets Clifton, once, twice, thrice, sometimes up to eighteen or nineteen times, until, fatigued and frustrated, the guy guarding you would let up mentally for a split second, allowing you to lay the ball—er, socks—up and in. And the prolific scoring would go on and on, despite the unyielding, grinding defense. And so would the silent groaning and moaning and sweating and bruising and pushing and pulling and bumping and grinding. Until, after four hours, exhausted, spent, and collapsed in a massive heap in the middle of his bedroom, Jimmy and I would at last agree to call it quits at 662–662.

Since that innocent time in the late fifties, my mind has often drifted back to that joyful game of sock and hanger in Jimmy Blumstein's bedroom, always evoking within me a knowing and affectionate smile. Except for one thing: as I age gracefully, it occurs to me increasingly (and sadly) that the phenomenon, why, the very *idea* of hangerball—much more than pre-marital sex or dress code or politics—represents the ultimate wedge between fathers and sons, the ultimate symbol of the proverbial "generation gap." Because I'd venture to say that no matter where the game is played today across this great country of ours (and I have no doubt that its like has been concocted by countless hyperactive members of the present generation), fathers are still objecting to the noise, the dirtying of socks, and, above all, the scratching and removal of door and transom paint by the scraping of coathangers.

And all of this familial divisiveness caused by a simple piece of wire, a humble lump of cotton, and an innocent childlike desire to satisfy the noble and timeless urge to do battle with a willing opponent!

Two Willies

For decades, particularly during the period when I was striding haughtily through the halls of academe, I was under the mistaken impression that most of the great quotes for the ages emanated from the domain of literature. Actually, I still think that there are some real nifty ones that can be sifted from reading the classics, the works of the Masters. But with all due respect, and after all is said and done, gimme a great quote from the world of sports anytime.

At the absolute Olympian summit of all-time sports quotes sits one manufactured by that great actress and even greater Giants fan, Tallulah Bankhead: "There have been only two geniuses in the world. Willie Mays and Willie Shakespeare."

The quote is a work of genius proportions for several reasons and needs to be admired at leisure. First, by its clever use of hyperbole, it brings attention to the real genius that Willie Mays possessed. Obviously, there were other geniuses "in the world"! But, implies Tallulah (*"there have been only two . . ."*), there are geniuses, *and there are geniuses.* And just as Shakespeare wasn't only good at writing for the theater but in fact *was* the theater, Mays wasn't only good at playing baseball, he *was* baseball.

Second, in her heart, she really, truly equates the genius of these two geniuses! Now any rational person, one might think, would respond that it's hard to equate (or even to mention in the same breath) the most brilliant ballplayer ever with the most brilliant *writer* ever. But using which criteria? Contributions to mankind? Importance in the scheme of the cosmos? For Tallulah (as for any die-hard Giants fan), Mays was every bit as much a genius as his sixteenth-century counterpart! Like Shakespeare, he could create drama (some would say poetry) of the highest order; he had a great flair for the extraordinary moment (the impossible catch and the doubling up of Cox at the plate in '51, the over-the-head catch off Wertz in '54, to name but two); he practiced his craft with enthusiasm (even glee) and developed an innovative style that was his alone (his double imprimatur of basket-catch and losing-of-cap-while-sliding); and he possessed "the whole package" of versatility (Leo's five-pointed star of fielding, throwing, running, hitting, and hitting with power). All of which explains Tallulah's conscious (and uproarious) use of *Willie* as the Bard's first name.

Finally, maybe it's timing or chance or some star shining in the distant heavens, but how else can you explain the fact that these two eminent geniuses among geniuses *just happened to have the same first name*? Tallulah was keenly sensitive of this star-crossed coincidence and was quick to pounce on it. Not only that, but consider how many other great Willies there have been, among whom these two had to be culled! Why, in basketball alone, there are plenty to choose from, including (off the top of my head) three of the greatest centers ever (Willie Russell, Willie Chamberlain, Willie Walton) and three of the greatest Knicks ever (Willie Naulls, Willie Reed, Willie Bradley). In tennis, Willie Tilden was arguably the greatest player of all time, and his rivalry with Little Willie Johnston arguably the most intense and long-standing ever. (Not to mention the greatest poet/tennis player ever, Willie Vilas.) For poetry in motion on the football field, who comes to mind after Gale Sayers? Willie Galimore! For poetry on the putting green, after Bobby Locke? Willie Casper! On the baseball diamond, what trio of first-sackers would you rather have than Willie McCovey, Willie Clark, and Willie White? For hittin' 'em where they ain't, who was better than the wee one, Willie Keeler? Who was the greatest jockey of all time? (Hint: Willie Shoemaker.) And the greatest billiard player? (Hint: Willie Mosconi.) I could go on and on, because there were also many, many great Willies outside of the realm of sports. Who was the greatest archer, for instance? Willie Tell, of course! And the greatest conqueror? Why, Willie the Conqueror! The greatest Kaiser? Kaiser Willie! The greatest creator of candies? Willie Wonka! And we haven't even begun to discuss all the other great writers accompanying the Bard in the pantheon of literary figures: Willie Blake, Willie Wordsworth, Willie Apollinaire, Willie Faulkner, Willie Yeats, and, of course, the second greatest writer/physician ever (just behind Frankie Rabelais), Willie Carlos Williams.

I actually find it mildly ironic that it took a woman—once and for all and definitively—to place Mays on that exalted pedestal, far from the madding crowd of would-be genius ballplayers. By comparing him pithily to the Bard, she has—brilliantly and with great perspicacity—brought to the attention of mankind just how special and different he was in the context of playing the game of baseball.

I don't know about you, but every time I see her quote, it positively gives me the Willies.

Two Impostors

In this great and bounteous country of ours, at the two poles of the sporting spectrum, we have compelling quotations, two roads diverging in a yellow wood and both available to us as fans and participants. In the blue corner, weighing in at 240 pounds, Vince Lombardi's:

Winning isn't everything; it's the only thing.

And in the red corner, weighing in at 165 pounds, Rudyard Kipling's:

If you can meet with Triumph and Disaster
And treat those two impostors just the same . . .

The choice is ours, individually and collectively. Two roads, two mentalities. As people or as a people, we can opt for the Dictum of the American Professional Athlete: win at any cost, avoid losing at any cost, preserve your macho pride, look at the Bottom Line, success and nothing less. Or the kinder, gentler choice: give it your best shot, and take both winning and losing in stride, with a grain of salt, with humility. It's *agape* vs. *hubris*, modesty vs. arrogance, total effort vs. raw results.

But before you rush to judgment, first a pop quiz. Mark an "x" in the boxes of those athletes you consider "winners," and leave blank the boxes of those athletes you consider "losers." O.K., begin:

- ❏ Bill Buckner
- ❏ Dan Jansen
- ❏ Ralph Branca
- ❏ Greg Norman
- ❏ Mary Decker Slaney
- ❏ Ernie Banks
- ❏ Ben Hogan
- ❏ Wilt Chamberlain
- ❏ Pat Riley
- ❏ Johnny Unitas
- ❏ The Buffalo Bills

O.K., pencils down. Well, guess what: you're wrong!

Fact is, all of the above are, without exception, *both* winners and losers. On the one hand, you can make an argument for all of them being "winners." Buckner batted .289 lifetime with 1208 RBIs and was one of the premier fielding first-sackers of his time. Jansen was (after Eric Heiden) probably the greatest male American speedskater ever. Branca won twenty-one games for Brooklyn in 1947 and had a very respectable career record of 88–68. Norman is, and has been for a while, one of the very greatest active golfers. Slaney ranks among the most successful female long-distance runners America has ever produced. Banks was maybe the greatest all-around shortstop ever to play the American pastime. Injury-free, Hogan may have been the greatest golfer ever (Tiger and The Golden Bear included). Wilt was the greatest offensive force in the history of basketball. Riley had one of the most impressive records, both as player and coach, in the annals of roundball. In some minds (mine included), Unitas—yeah, yeah,

Montana and Elway were pretty good too—was the greatest clutch QB in history. And no franchise got to the Super Bowl in the nineties more often than the Bills.

Of course, in a sense, you'd also be within your rights to label all of the above as "losers" too. Buckner will forever be remembered for letting that squibber hit by Mookie Wilson dribble through his legs in Game 6 of the '86 Series. Jansen, of course, was a huge disappointment to all, blowing his Golden Chances in the '92 Olympics. Branca, well, just look up what happened in the old Polo Grounds at 3:58 P.M. on October 3, 1951. Norman lost all those majors, and who can forget his collapse during the final round of the Faldo-won '96 Masters? Slaney fell down like a rank amateur in the most important race of her life. Banks toiled for the Cubs: ergo, he never wore a World Series ring. Hogan was embarrassed by the unknown Jack Fleck in the playoff of the '55 U.S. Open. Wilt lost most of those Championship series to Russell and the Celtics; and, before that, in '57, his Jayhawks lost a triple-overtime NCAA final to UNC. In '66, Riley and his Kentucky Wildcat teammates found themselves on the short end of the most embarrassing upset in the history of the NCAAs. Replacing Morrall, Unitas just didn't have it, as he and his Colts were embarrassed by Namath and the upstart Jets in the '69 Super Bowl. And the Bills went to the Super Bowl four times in a row and came in second four times in a row.

My point is that every athlete who *ever* competed, at any level, is both winner *and* loser. That both winning and losing are fleeting, and it's usually not a great idea to hold either one on a pedestal or in awe. That there's a fine line between success and failure in sports (as in life, of course) and that to place too much emphasis on results may be harmful to your health. That, as ol' Rudyard suggested, victory and defeat are indeed impostors, posing as a false sense of self-pride and merit on the one hand and a false sense of inadequacy and unworthiness on the other.

Now don't get me wrong: I'll concede that deep down, we all want to win. There's no crime in that: it's a perfectly natural urge. And if you and I meet on a tennis court or a golf course or a playground with a hoop, my first impulse is to beat your bones to a pulp. But it's a question of to what extent we *lust* for victory and *fear* defeat. I mean, in the final analysis, *how much does it really matter?*

Now if winning is the only goal, the be-all and end-all of competition, we have to consider the consequences. What happens to the unfettered joy of competing? What happens to all the lessons we learn from losing? What happens to rivalries built on respect for our opponents, win or lose? On the pro level alone, look what we've lost through our "win-at-any-cost" mentality. What ever became of those teams we used to root for and who had the same roster year after year? What ever became of those athletes who used to *smile* because they loved competing? Will the Willie Mayses and Magic Johnsons of this world be permanently replaced by the Deion Sanderses and the Dennis Rodmen? Will Ernie Banks' celebrated quote be mangled to read, *Let's play two, if the price is right?*

No sirree, when it comes to sizing up the ultimate value of winning and losing, it's impossible for both Kipling and Lombardi to be right.

Sorry, Vince.

The Saga of Blaise and Ickey

It's funny how certain lofty, deeply philosophical pronouncements are so profoundly appropriate as they relate to the domain of sports. Take Blaise Pascal's quote on the insignificance of man in the context of the cosmos, for example: *The eternal silence of these infinite spaces terrifies me.*

Believe it or not, I was contemplating this very quote recently as I was scuba diving at Molokini, a small horseshoe-shaped crater off the southwestern coast of Maui. Being ninety feet below the water surface does funny things to the ego: cruising among the white-tip sharks, rays, sea turtles, eels, fishes, corals, nudebranchs, and anemones gives a body the decided feeling of relative insignificance in the presence of such a glorious and admirable panoply of creatures. In fact, it's probably one of the most humbling experiences one can have, inside or outside the sporting arena.

So there I am, bathing (literally) in humility, in this huge expanse of liquid space inhabited by mobile miracles, and quietly admiring the wisdom of a quote from a great seventeenth-century French thinker, when suddenly, boisterously, and from out of the blue, the image of Ickey Woods doing his celebratory Bengalese end-zone "shuffle" appears before me, exploding the grace and serenity of the moment into smithereens with its raucous, hyperkinetic jukes of self-adulation.

I'm not certain why it was specifically Ickey who appeared before me at that precise moment. Perhaps a linguistic coincidence ("Ickey" being a second cousin to "ichthyology")? But what was clear is that Ickey surely represents an extreme example of what is at the other end of the spectrum to the humility in which I was submerged. And my subconscious must have summoned him from the depths to make a point: in this wonderful world in which we humans are but an infinitesimal part of the whole picture, how can someone like Ickey Woods happen?

Ickey Woods and the humbling nature of existence as we know it. It's a strange juxtaposition, perhaps equivalent to how our species could have spawned phenomena as antipodal as Mozart and Snoop Doggi Dog or even Joe Louis and Mike Tyson. And the more I thought about Ickey's annoying antics, the more I mourned the recent and regrettable loss of humility in the world of sports.

Remember the clip of the Clipper gently kicking the dirt near second base just after Al Gionfriddo robbed him of that homer in the '47 Series? That was considered the only time when the classy DiMag ever "lost it"! Now compare that relatively innocuous outburst with some of the many examples of recent stridency—Ickey's shuffle, Ali's merciless taunting of Liston, Reggie Miller's "trash-talking," Jack McDowell's flipping the bird to the Yankee Stadium crowd, Roberto Alomar's expectorating into John Hirschbeck's face, Dennis Rodman's kicking a photographer—and you'll begin to appreciate just how low we've sunk.

Now, part of me wants to understand and appreciate the exuberance of some of these "sporting gestures." I mean, is it a crime to let off steam, to find catharsis in a stressful profession? And, in Ickey's case, isn't he just following in a modern tradition that began with Homer Jones' self-expressive spiking, continued with the animated terpsichorean shenanigans of Elmo Wright and Billy "White Shoes" Johnson, and culminated with today's chest-banging, elbow-smashing, end-zone-exploding behavioral hyperkinesis? After all, what's wrong with self-expression, ebullience, and joyful merry-making?

Actually, the question isn't rhetorical: let me *tell* you what's wrong with all this nonsense. Personally, what I don't like about it is not what it is, but what it *isn't*. What we've lost is the inner pride of accomplishment, the classy, private, low-key, laid-back way of celebrating. In a nutshell, I dearly miss watching Jim Brown struggle his way into the end-zone and place the ball on the ground. *Period*. We all knew what he just did, and above all, he knew too. No need to "show the world" or to brag or to say: *look at me!* The act of reaching the end-zone (or, for that matter, hitting it into the stands or serving an ace or draining a twenty-foot snake or hitting the winning free throws) used to be an end in itself. In a word, the old, honorable concept of *facta non verba* (deeds, not words) has—presto!—vanished into thin air.

I dunno, maybe it's the money they're all making nowadays (the traditional rationale). Or the breakdown of "family values" (the Republican rationale). Or the elimination of Latin and Greek from the high school curriculum (my rationale). All of the above are, in the end, just excuses for a deeper, more fundamental absence: who plays the game for the pure, inner joy of it any more? Oh, there are exceptions (whom, sadly, we call "throwbacks"). And hopefully, there will always be the Magic Johnsons and the Michael Jordans and the Cal Ripkens and the Tony Gwynns and the Marcus Allens and the Barry

Sanderses and the Pete Samprases and the Stefan Edbergs of this world, talented performers who take pride in their work and don't care about rubbing their opponents' noses in it.

But if a group of youngsters were to accost me and ask what they could do about this sad state of affairs and how to gain some perspective for their own lives, I'm not sure I'd be wise enough to dole out any meaningful advice. Maybe I'd tell them to take a clue from the athletes I mentioned above. Or from almost *anyone* on the PGA or LPGA or Senior PGA tour. Or maybe I'd send them to the sports archives to view films of the old ballplayers, to watch the joy of Willie Mays and Dr. J., the humble grace of Joe D. and Gale Sayers, the intense stylishness of Stan the Man and Johnny U., the mutual respect and sportsmanship of all those great old Aussie tennis players.

Or maybe, just maybe, I'd simply tell them to grab some scuba gear, get certified, hop a plane to Maui, go out on a dive boat, and descend about ninety feet to where all those awesome creatures are doing their thing. And then, when they're nice and relaxed, to summon to their humbled consciousness that wonderful old quote of Pascal's.

Kennebec Claybox

It's not that I don't enjoy playing tennis on other surfaces. Far from it: I'm comfortable on a rubberized hard court, enjoy carpet thoroughly, thrive on Har-Tru, and absolutely adore grass. But give me a choice between any of these and clay, and I'll choose the red stuff every time.

Ah, clay! Pure, thick, dense, natural, rich, ruby, red, vermilion, gritty, grainy, gravelly, soft, slippy, slidey clay! Even talking about the stuff makes me feel giddy. Goofy. Silly-billy, goo-goo, ga-ga, yessirree Bob, *wheeeeeeeeeee*!

(Sorry.)

Anyhow, I just *love* clay, maybe because, to my mind, it offers tennis fanatics the truest test of their ability, allowing them to grind it out (endurance), put all kinds of spin on the ball (shot-making), think out a point and move their opponents around the court (strategy), and react to various kinds of bounces (reflexes). Or—on a more personal note—maybe because it's a great equalizer, allowing shorter, smaller, less physical players to hang in there against bigger, more

powerful opponents with their oversized, overpowering, hi-tech racquets. And it's so incredibly sensuous, in terms of its color, its rich-
ness, its texture. Then there is its regenerative nature: its ability to dig
itself up and then put itself back together, to be drenched in rain and
to dry out in no time. It's also a truly just and democratic surface, one
on which you can actually see the mark left by a tennis ball and thus
prove to an umpire or an opponent that the ball was in or out. Not
to mention the fact that it lets you slide into a shot, giving you a
sense of grace and smoothness (and, not unimportantly, saving you
from unspeakable foot, leg, and groin injuries). And, to top it all off,
you get the stuff caked and smeared all over your socks and shirt and
shorts and wristlet and sneakers and you end up looking like you've
really earned your keep.

Furthermore, pros who play the circuit generally agree that the
French Open at Roland Garros and the Italian Open at the Foro
Italico are the most grueling tests on their schedule. Round after
round of five-setters on clay with those European baseliners is
enough to debilitate even the best-conditioned, hardest-serving physical specimens on tour!

One of my fondest tennis memories regarding this surface was an
annual summer tennis tournament, the Kennebec Invitational at
Camp Kennebec in Maine, in which I played from 1958–60. Partly
because I won it three times. Partly because of the new friends I
made from the different camps and the keen competition it provided.
But mostly because of the clay.

Kennebec was a well-run camp that specialized in two sports:
swimming and tennis. Their basketball and baseball teams were always
pretty good, but the level of their tennis and swimming programs was
virtually unparalleled. And they really knew how to throw a tennis
tournament! The people at the camp took real pride in having everything run smoothly, with no hitches: I can't remember a match ever
running late or having to be delayed or even an on-court argument;

everyone was always eager to follow the rules; the linesmen and umpires were all counselors from the host camp, and all amazingly fair-minded.

Then there were the crowds. (Yes, *crowds* at a boys' summer camp!) The courts were set up in the middle of two rows of tents; and on each side of the courts, from one end to the other, kids would sit at the edge of the tents, with their legs dangling over, and watch the matches, cheer, applaud good shots, go crazy.

But it's the clay that I remember most. The courts were kept in immaculate condition, watered several times a day, groomed magnificently, rolled and swept daily. The quality of the clay was as good or better than any I've seen, before or since. Anywhere in the world. It was rich and thick and smooth, and you could slide into your shots (if your technique was good) with the effortless grace of a Pietrangeli or a Santana or a Leconte.

Actually, what I remember most about the Kennebec tournament was *the claybox*. Near Court #1, there was this huge green wooden box inside which were stored mounds and mounds of excess clay, to be used to fill in gaps, to augment the surface when it got a bit thin, or for general resurfacing. I loved this box and would open it furtively from time to time each day to examine the forbidden rich red mounds of stuff (ostensibly, to be used only by the Kennebec tennis staff), even take some in my hands when no one was looking and mush it around with my eyes closed, slowly and lovingly, enjoying its color and texture. What I *really* enjoyed doing, though, was to sneak over to the box in the still of the night, when the whole camp was asleep, smoosh clay all over the surface of my sneakers (the first two years they were Converses, the last year Jack Purcells), and leave them there to "ferment" overnight. Then I'd go back the next morning before my match, take them out (by now, they were deliciously smeared and completely caked with the red stuff), and put them on prior to setting out to do battle. I recall, especially during my last summer there (1960), the warrior-like feeling they'd give me while I was warming up, the pleasant sensations of toughness and virility and fearlessness and invincibility.

Now that I think of it, what an incredible coincidence! Weren't these the precise qualities made famous, the same summer in Rome, by that most amazing of all athletes, a guy named Cassius Marcellus . . . what's his name?

Siblings at the Pipidrome

This is a story that has *everything*. A touching family drama. Plenty of conflict. Excitement and high-speed action. A harrowing climax. A happy ending. And one more thing. It's not about baseball or basketball or football or hockey or soccer or tennis or golf or any of those "major" sports; rather, it's quite possibly the first story ever written about the sadly-neglected athletic event of frog racing.

It all happened on Forth-ninth Street in Brooklyn, where my family lived during most of the fifties. There, in the middle of a deeply Hasidic neighborhood, stood #1270, a two-story brick house, in which my family lived and where my father conducted his medical practice.

His office was in the front of the house, surrounded by two examining rooms and a pathology laboratory. It was there that my older brother Stephen and I discovered the excitement, challenge, and joys of a brand new sport.

Now, you must understand at the outset how different we were as children. By the time I reached my first consciousness of the world around me, he had firmly established himself as the bearer of the family "brain baton." Yes, it was he who would carry the familial cerebral torch into the sixties and beyond. And the fact became clear in our home (and for miles around) that *he* was the student, *he* was the brain, *he* was the reader, *he* was the academic, *he* was the smart one. (Oh, pipe down! Who ever told you life was *fair?*) So, since this particular (intellectual) avenue of endeavor was already "taken" by him, I decided to distinguish myself in athletics, an avenue with which—owing both to his intense preoccupation with the pursuit of knowledge and his particular gene pool—he was singularly unfamiliar. And so it was that he spent the preponderance of his time inside reading and preparing for life and I the preponderance of mine outside in the driveway playing with my Spaldeen and preparing for life.

As we essentially occupied two separate and unmergeable worlds, I can't remember his ever coming out to play with me and, thus, to share the passion and joys of athletic competition with his younger brother.

That all ended with a crash the night we discovered *the frogs.*

So we're poking around in Dad's laboratory one evening (against the house rules, but, after all, we were *kids*). Walking fearlessly past the racks of test tubes and that centrifuge machine that spun them around and around and all the microscopes and the piles of slides and Petri dishes and pipettes and Erlenmeyer flasks and jars of alcohol and cotton wads and such, we finally reach the refrigerator that stood at the entrance of the lab. As we open it, our eyes pan down the various bottles and dishes and lab samples until they reach the "Crisper" section, whence a strange sound is emanating. Upon further examination, we determine it to be the croaking of frogs.

Frogs!

Can you *imagine* what discovering a whole mess of frogs in a refrigerator means to a couple of idiot kids poking around for something mischievous to do in their father's off-limits lab on a weekday night? Why, it's a proverbial gold mine! The pot of coins at the end of the rainbow! The Promised Land!

(You may be wondering at this point why the hell there were frogs in the fridge in the first place. Well, at that point in time, it's what pathologists were using for pregnancy tests. They'd inject the frogs with a woman's urine, then squeeze the liquid out of the frog and onto a slide. *Don't ask.* Anyway, my father told us the hilarious story of how they got there: he'd send a technician to pick up this cardboard box filled with these frogs—they were African—from some storehouse, and the technician would return via the BMT subway line among a crush of people, holding this stupid croaking box, and the people wouldn't know what the hell was in there and some would laugh and some would run away like the guy was holding the goddam Black Plague or something. Dad kept the frogs floating in water in the "Crisper" compartment: I guess they kept fresh for the tests that way. Again, *don't ask.*)

So there we are, these ridiculous grins plastered on our faces as we survey the swimming, kicking, croaking beasts. In a split-second, our creative, infantile minds kick into gear, and immediately and nearly without hesitation, we know what has to be done.

Frog races!

We quietly remove two beauties (we would choose our individual "racers" with great deliberation, checking out their appearances to determine which ones had the most speed, endurance, and pliability, as if either of us had the slightest inkling of what the hell he was doing), cup them in our hands, and walk to the edge of the lab. The starting line would be the threshold between the vestibule (the fancy word for foyer in those days) and the lab, the point at which the orange linoleum of the vestibule ended and the black-and-white squares of the lab linoleum began. The tension is thick, mostly because of our fear that the croaking would attract the attention of our parents, who were probably upstairs reading or watching Uncle Miltie or doing God Knows What.

Stephen, being a budding scholar of words, languages, facts, and basically anything that had to do with knowledge, informs me that the Latin for frog is *rana pipiens* and that, consequently, we should dub the raceway "pipidrome," or "frog arena," a clever variation, of course, on the ancient, hippodromous (equine) track.

We both kneel down at the starting line of the pipidrome, make some tooting sounds that vaguely resemble ancient Roman trumpets, and then, in loud, throaty whispers, bark out in unison the starting instructions to our frogs (the pipiatic parallel to Indy's "Gentlemen, start your engines!"): *"Plunk your magic twanger, froggy!"* (It's the exact command given to that strange character, Froggy, from the old "Andy Devine Show" on TV.)

At this very moment, we drop our frogs simultaneously, and the race begins! Actually, it'll end up being a very exciting sporting event, but for the moment, there are our two frogs, webbed feet stuck at the starting line, as if someone had applied a wad of Lepage's glue there. Stupefied. In complete and total shock. For some reason, I suppose we assumed that they'd automatically or instinctively know they were in a competitive mode and would have some inkling of what to do.

Nothing.

We quickly learn about the "prodding" technique, however; and once we do, the action picks up considerably, with both of us (in our adolescent innocence) prodding, tickling, plinking, or otherwise cajoling our slimy charges to inch (or millimeter) their way forward toward The Finish Line. And when one of them does (after about a half-hour of mad, wild, and exhausting cajoling by their "trainers"), there is general rejoicing by the winner and sour-sport, sore-loser petulant objection by the loser. I think the races ended up being pretty even, with each brother winning and losing about equally.

I have no idea how we kept this intense competition a secret from our parents. Perhaps we didn't and they were smarter than we'd given them credit for. At any rate, we continue the races surreptitiously for weeks and weeks, sneaking down to the lab night after night, opening the fridge, selecting our "frogs of the night," then prodding and cajoling them at the ol' pipidrome. Until one fateful evening, when, at the climax of one of the tightest, most hotly-contested frog races of all time, one of our creatures hops past The Finish Line and . . . *disappears!*

To this day, neither of us can recall precisely whose frog it was. No matter. The whole sleazy affair ends, however, several days later, when a fetid, putrefying odor begins to waft throughout the kitchen. I think our mother had smelled something "not right" and then, to her horror, discovers the sweltering, smoldering, rancid, cooked cadaver of the wretched *rana*. Right there smooshed behind the radiator and the wall, beneath the kitchen window. To her credit, she handles it rather diplomatically (and with typical maternal protectiveness), promising us she wouldn't tell our father about it but urging us in the sweetest way imaginable to put an immediate halt to this particular hobby.

Through the years, I've often wondered how in the world the frog made its way from the lab to the kitchen without being detected by either parent or any of the lab technicians or patients. I mean, compared to the "magic bullet" of the JFK assassination, the route this frog would have had to take was positively frightening. It would have had to exit the lab by hanging a sharp right, jump across the carpeted floor of our father's private office, continue through the long hallway that went past the examining rooms, hang a ralph at the bathroom, then hang a quick louie over the threshold and into the kitchen, and then hop across the entire length of the kitchen and make a right under the dining table and under the radiator! I'm guessing it must have had to travel only during the dead of night, when we were all asleep, holing up under some table or in some remote corner as soon as dawn broke so as not to be discovered in broad daylight.

Quite frankly, I don't think I'll ever be able to figure out what really happened to it. But then again, frogs move in mysterious ways.

Tennis Lessons

I fell in love with the game of tennis in 1951, when I was nearly seven years old. Ironically, that was The Year The Giants Won The Pennant: by rights, there should have been no room in my heart for any other sport but baseball. But my older brother began taking tennis lessons that year, and I was jealous that he was taking them and not me, so (after much whining, no doubt) I roped my parents into letting me take them too.

I learned the game from a pro named Bill Thompson, an old Irish guy (he seemed around seventy to my seven-year-old eyes) who gave lessons at the old Regiment Armory in Brooklyn. Bill was hypercasual and slow afoot but nonetheless a terrific teacher. The other things I remember about him: he was a lefty with looping strokes, played with a red Wilson Top Notch racquet, always wore the same outfit (a sort of throwback costume: thick V-neck white tennis sweater with a thick red-and-blue "V" pattern at the neck;

145

long white trousers; Converse sneakers), and was always tremendously encouraging.

Since the lessons with Bill, I have played the game lovingly and faithfully my entire life and have had some wonderful memories connected with it over the past forty-seven years. Including playing on the Eastern junior circuit (ELTA) and in summer-camp tournaments; competing on my high school and college teams; teaching and coaching in the U.S., France, and Israel; playing against a Davis Cup doubles team from Chile (two of the Gildemeister brothers) in a pro charity tournament; and spending six days at a fantasy camp with John Newcombe and the Legends. I've played on grass, carpet, clay, dirt, wood, Har-Tru, asphalt, and all kinds of synthetics, from rubber to cement. On courts from Palm Beach to Palm Springs, from Barcelona to Besançon, from Rio to Ramat Hasharon, from Maui to Montreal. And the game has allowed me to meet some incredible human beings, develop some wonderful friendships and rivalries, and have some of the best times of my life. But most of all, through the years, it has taught me *lessons*. Not the kind I got from Bill Thompson on the subjects of groundstrokes, footwork, and mental focus, but the kind I got from struggle and setbacks in regard to self-improvement, self-esteem, and self-knowledge.

I. NIEDERHOFFER!

My first big tennis lesson came from my first big loss. (Ever since, I've become more and more conscious of the fact that you learn infinitely more from losing than from winning.) As a pre-teen, I had been thoroughly enjoying the thrill of victory, when, at the age of 13, I enter an ELTA junior tournament at the Hi-Way Courts (red clay) in Brooklyn. I think it was in the quarters that I am pitted against a kid named Victor Niederhoffer, and little did I know then that I was to be given a lesson by the Tennis Gods that would remain with me all my life and probably go with me to the grave. And nothing Bill

Thompson ever taught me (nor Elwood Cooke nor Martin Buxby nor John Nogrady nor Julie Copeland) could have prepared me for what was to occur on that bleak Saturday morning.

I arrive on time for the match: punctuality, like wearing the proper attire, was a given in those days. So there I am, standing at the drawsheet area, dressed in appropriate tennies (white Fred Perry shirt, pleated cream-colored shorts, white wristlet, white socks, white Converses), waiting dutifully. And waiting. And just when it looks like my opponent will be defaulted, there appears on the scene a human being who seems as likely to be entered in a tennis tournament as a Halloween trick-or-treater. He is bedecked in a loud, striped polo shirt, shiny red basketball trunks, and very old black Chuck Taylor high-top sneakers in desperate need of a re-tread. I learn that it is he. *Niederhoffer!* On top of his wretched, unruly, unkempt attire, he has this strange, left-handed (read: sinister, gauche) manner about him, as if something were just a bit off: hunched-up posture, far-away look in the eye, sneering mien. Lanky, emaciated, with his concave chest and spindly legs, he doesn't even look *vaguely* like an athlete, much less a human being.

And to top it all off, he refuses to shake hands!

As we walk onto our assigned court, I have the Gordian Knot wedged in the pit of my stomach. *How the hell can I play this guy? What an embarrassment! What a schmuck!*

We warm up, and rather than assess his strengths and weaknesses, I'm still dumbstruck at the *chutzpah* he has to dress up like that. *Why, the nerve!* And then, suddenly, I notice something else very bizarre about this kid: he's ambidextrous! I mean, he's hitting forehands on both wings! The kid doesn't have a backhand! *What the hell?*

The match begins, but at the very outset, I'm not myself. I'm not playing "my shots" or exploiting his weaknesses or hitting out or doing anything that I'm used to doing. He's a consummate player, a wonderful athlete, a brilliant shotmaker. But at the same time, he has the most unorthodox, lunging strokes imaginable, he's gawky and ungainly, crass and snide and snotty and surly. He has no etiquette, he makes silent calls, he skulks, he sulks, he fumes, he shows me no respect. And most of all, he has succeeded in getting into my head. So this is all I can think about:

1. What a schmuck this guy is.
2. What a jerk this guy is.
3. How idiotic he looks.
4. How bad his form is.
5. How much better I look.
6. How much better my form is.
7. How much better behaved I am.
8. How badly I should be beating him.
9. How much better a player I am.
10. How much better a person I am.

There are, of course, few details about the match I have retained after forty years. I do know that I kept the first set close (I think it was 7–5) only because I was very quick and able to run down everything, and because I had lots of heart: I'd *die* before I'd give up on a point or, for that matter, a match. But I also know that even early on, I was only playing with my body: my mind was on sabbatical, thousands of miles away from the action. I know that the second set was all downhill, and that when it was all over, I felt really crappy losing to this son-of-a-bitch, awkward, surly, ambidextrous bastard!

But I also know that this match taught me, in the long run, what competitive tennis is all about. That you shouldn't be obsessed with beating the guy across the net from you, but rather about playing your best and concentrating on the game. That form is nice, but what really counts is performance. That two wrongs don't make a right, and that you should respect your opponent for his strengths

and his effort, regardless of his behavior. That playing well and trying your best is all the reward you could ask for. And I also learned
about that old Zen teaching that you shouldn't step in other people's shit.

Funny enough, I later discovered that I must've been only one
of many, many people who had to learn these difficult lessons from
this guy. About five years later, when I was playing squash for
Williams College, we were at Harvard, and who was their number
one player? *Niederfhoffer!* Turns out he'd become a top squash player
after only barely learning the game. And he's pulling the same crap
with our number one player (a wonderful athlete named Mike
Annison), skulking and sulking and sneering, and still winning! And
a few years later, I'm reading a *Sports Illustrated* article about this guy
who'd become the number two player *in the world*, ahead of three or
four Khans (which is akin to my starting in the San Francisco
Giants' outfield ahead of one of the Alou brothers). And his name?
Niederhoffer! Indeed, despite his antics and behavior and style, this
guy turns out to be one of the great natural athletes I've ever seen.
And about *forty* years later, I'm reading this book review in the *New
York Times* about this Wall Street speculator who's made a killing out
of his fiduciary brilliance accompanied by a pompous, arrogant,
sneering, boorish egomania.

Sound familiar?

And so, I raise my glass to you, Niederhoffer, wherever you may
be. In spite of the patronizing, supercilious way in which you handled
others, you *did* nonetheless perform one good deed: unwittingly, you
taught me some valuable lessons about competing, coping with
demons, and focusing on what really counts. I know forty years after
the fact is a bit late to be making a toast of gratitude, but I hope you
can find it in your heart to forgive me.

L'hayyim!

II. ME AND SISYPHUS

From 1975 to 1981, I developed a wonderful tennis rivalry with David Frantz, a professor of English at Ohio State. Through the years, we not only became close friends, but we spent many, many hours on the tennis court, in club matches and tournaments, on private and university courts, as doubles partners and doubles opponents, and playing singles.

The singles matches were particularly memorable: always fun, hotly contested, and very close. We ran down every ball, had excruciatingly long rallies, tried every shot in the book, and raised the level of both our games every time we took the court. And it was during our long rivalry that I learned one of the great lessons the game of tennis can teach.

As it happened, there was one overriding aspect of our rivalry that was especially noticeable: the final tally-sheet. Now, if I told you that we had both started playing at very tender ages, that we were both brought up on Eastern tennis (mostly clay), that we had both played a gazillion tournament matches through the years, that our games were pretty similar, that we both relied on steadiness and foot speed and court coverage and strategy, that we had pretty similar physiques (he was 5'8" and 145, I was 5'7" and 155), and that we probably played, oh, eighty singles matches against each other over the years, what would you guess the final standings would be?

Wrong.

Fact is, in all those matches, I beat David a grand total of *twice*. Fact is, his game was just a little bit stronger, just a little bit more powerful, just a little steadier, just a little bit more aggressive.

I mean, it was amazing! Almost without exception, every match went either three close sets or two close sets, often tie-breakers. There were very few lop-sided matches, maybe a couple at most. But, in a nutshell, David won the great majority of big points, when it counted. And after the first dozen or so times we played, I realized the simple fact that, as close and exciting as our matches always seemed to be, he was, pure and simple, the better player.

All of which didn't make me fight any less gallantly; on the contrary, I remember clawing my way back from large deficits many times, only to be repelled at the end. I always got the most out of my game and had that great feeling that I had played well, had given it my entire effort, and, together with David, had produced some wonderful moments on the court.

But the fact remains that, with the exception of those two times that I won, the outcome of our matches, as they wound down to their conclusion, was nearly a foregone one: David would be the one who was just that much better. Funny thing is, the times I won, I didn't really feel any different. Really! No special joy or exultation or feeling of accomplishment. Rather, the same feeling of playing well and enjoying a close, fun match.

Which is where Sisyphus comes in. (I bet you were wondering.)

As you may recall, Sisyphus was condemned by the gods to an eternal, hopeless torture. His particular punishment was to roll a huge boulder up a mountain, at the top of which the boulder would inevitably roll back down to the bottom, forcing him to descend and roll the boulder back up the mountain. Ad infinitum.

From the first time I ever heard about his tragic plight in Bob Pasotti's high school Ancient History course to the first time I read Albert Camus' philosophical essay (*Le Mythe de Sisyphe*) in one of Jack Savacool's seminars at Williams, I'd always been fascinated by the metaphorical power of this tale. The Camus tract was particularly thought-provoking: he presented Sisyphus not as a defeated figure, but as an "absurd" hero who, at the top of the mountain, experiences an epiphany, becomes conscious of his plight, and, rather than bow his head in hopelessness, rises above the very fate to which he is "doomed."

Indeed. But for me, as fascinating as it was, this story always existed on an abstract, intellectual level. I've often asked myself since: how could I, as a human being, learn from this myth and extract from it some practical value?

How about losing to the same opponent in seventy-eight out of eighty long, close, hard-fought tennis matches? Yes: it was during my long tennis rivalry with David Frantz that I too, like Sisyphus, reached a lucid understanding of my "ordeal," that I too found real meaning in *the struggle*.

But more important than being a lesson I learned from Sisyphus, this was one of the great lessons I learned from tennis. It is *the struggle* that counts, not the winning or the losing. It is the noble effort of rolling the rock that elevates us as human beings, not whether it stays at the top of the mountain or rolls back down. It is why sports in general, and tennis in particular, has within it such beauty and nobility. And why we can enjoy it and learn from it, whatever the outcome might be. But rather than stutter and stammer in my attempt to express the grandeur that is tennis, I should leave Camus, who said it (unbeknownst to him) more eloquently than I ever could, the last word:

> *I leave Sisyphus at the foot of the mountain, where his*
> *burden is constantly renewed! But Sisyphus teaches a*
> *higher loyalty, one that negates gods and upholds rocks.*
> *He also judges that all is well. This henceforth godless*
> *universe appears to him neither sterile nor futile. Each*
> *one of this stone's grains, every little mineral glitter of this*
> *pitch-black mountain represents an entire world to him*
> *alone. The very struggle toward the summits is enough to*
> *fill a man's heart. We must imagine Sisyphus happy.*

III. THE HEART OF THE MATTER

So, as it turns out in most triptychs, we have (not by chance) perfect symmetry: the first two great tennis lessons that I learned occurred in my teens and my thirties; and the final great one happened shortly after my fiftieth birthday.

Ah, fifty! For some, the number represents a new epoch in the continual process of the "aging of the wine." For others, it might be the time when grandchildren arrive or when thoughts of mortality first materialize or when gray hairs begin to congregate in earnest or when the mid-life crisis is here for good or when you get to say hi to your prostate or when you finally begin to see the light or when you finally get to belong to AARP. For me, it was all of these, but in particular, entering into my sixth decade on earth meant that I was at long last eligible to play in USTA senior tournaments. Yes: a new challenge, a clean slate, a chance to see how well I could compete with the best of those of us who were long in the tooth, over the hill, turning the corner.

But life is strange, and a funny thing happened on my way to fifty-one.

I'll never forget the day of my fiftieth birthday as long as I live. Several weeks before, I'd decided to move to California from the New York area. I'd just gone through a divorce, packed up my car with all my "valuables" (tennis racquets, rollerblades, a few important books, some pictures of my kids), and driven to Florida to spend a few weeks with my folks, play tennis with my old tennis-pro friend Mike Appelbaum, and decide where I was going to spend the rest of my life. From my final list of ten cities (Paris, London, Florence, Copenhagen, Barcelona, Boston, Seattle, Santa Fe, San Diego, San Francisco), I decide on the latter: great city, great weather, year-round tennis, a brother and a few friends who live in the area.

I leave for the Left Coast on November 3rd, having driven back up to New York, making a few stops along the way to visit friends. On that first day, I stop in Ithaca to visit my older daughter Jennifer at Cornell, then continue on, through a monsoon, to Joliet, IL. Day 2 takes me all the way to Cheyenne, WY. (I am really anxious to reach the Coast in four days; besides, the countryside, although breathtaking, doesn't invite stopping for any reasons other than eating and relieving myself.) And by the eve of November 5th, I make it all the way to Nevada, at which point a mammoth blizzard hits, nearly wiping me and my chainless Miata off the road several times. The visibility is about three inches, eighteen-wheelers are swerving all over the road, and better judgment tells me to check into a Motel 6 right then and there. Which is precisely where I awake the next morning, the very morn of my fiftieth birthday. So there I am, in frigging Winnemucka, Nevada, in the middle of a blizzard, heading dizzyingly toward a new life, a new city, a new profession, a new abode, a new beginning. Pretty scary stuff.

Anyway, the next few months are nothing short of amazing. Quickly and by chance, I find a wonderful apartment in Berkeley, up in the hills, with a fantastic view of the Berkeley campus and the entire Bay (Golden Gate Bridge, Alcatraz, San Francisco skyline). I resume a relationship with my brother that had lain fallow for nearly twenty years because we'd been living on opposite coasts (he'd been in Berkeley since the late seventies). I publish one book and begin serious work on two others. And, most important, I meet a wonderful woman I'd dated in college in 1965–66 (her older brother was one of my roommates at Williams, and during my senior year, Diane had come East to attend Skidmore). After all those years (twenty-nine, to be exact), we meet again, and I begin commuting regularly between my adopted Berkeley and her native Sonoma. Except for the fact that I am now 3200 miles from my kids and my pockets aren't exactly full, life is pretty good, considering the daunting challenges facing me only months before.

It is at this point, after things had pretty much settled down in my life, that I decide to enter my very first senior tournament. I'm in probably the best shape I'd been in since college, a result of daily rollerblading and tennis three times a week.

The tournament is held in Oakland at the Chabot Canyon Tennis Club, a fine facility I'd joined soon after I stepped foot in The Golden State. I'm fairly optimistic about my chances of doing well in the tournament, since I'd played Joe Morgan (yes, *that* Joe Morgan) a few weeks before: after leading 4–1, I end up losing the set in a tie-breaker. Joe is ranked #3 or 4 in Northern California, and I figure I could be pretty competitive in the seniors based on our result.

My first-round opponent is an Asian-American who has a game similar to mine: he's a baseliner who has decent power but who can run down everything. His strokes are extremely unorthodox, but he has a good strategic mind and is very strong mentally. At the outset, we're content to trade strokes, but after the first few games, it appears that I'm a bit stronger and steadier. I jump quickly to a 5–1 lead and feel good about my chances of winning the match handily. Then, at fifteen–love, while stretching for a shot, I feel this twinge in my left hamstring.

Uh-oh.

I can't believe it: my very first senior tournament, and I'm virtually unable to move easily and without pain! Try as I might to eke out another game, it is almost impossible. Like a shark smelling blood, my able opponent senses the kill and runs me all over the goddam court. In a flash, it's 5–2, then 5–4, then 6–5 his. Somehow, I manage to win another game, forcing the set into a tie-breaker. Now, why at this point I don't default, I can't tell you. Well, actually, yes I can. Reason dictated that even if I happen to win the set miraculously, there's no way on earth I can win another set, much less another game or two. It is hopeless, pointless. But who said Reason had anything to do with it? As usual, I invoke my favorite quote, you know, the one by Pascal: *The heart has its reasons that Reason doesn't have a clue about.* And, like an absolute idiot, I play on.

Winning that twelfth game had taken so much out of me that I am running on fumes for the tie-breaker. I think I lose it 7–2 or 7–3.

We rest between sets, but as I sit there slumped on my chair, I feel something terribly wrong. I *know* what it is (hint: it has nothing to do with my leg) but don't want to admit it and certainly don't want to throw in the towel as far as the match is concerned. After all, this is my first senior tournament! *What, you wait fifty years to enter it, and then you just give up? What, you're some kind of wuss? What, you get a little itty-bitty pain in your chest, and you wave the white flag?* I wait for three or four minutes, until it gets so bad that I finally tell my opponent I'm terribly sorry but have to default the match. After he leaves the court, I remain there for probably ten to fifteen minutes, unable to move. Pain in my chest. Radiating down my left arm. Classic. Yep, I'm having a mild heart attack. I hadn't had any problems since my quadruple-bypass operation nearly nine years earlier, so who expected any trouble? And if I had given in completely to my instincts (*never give up; keep on fighting, no matter what*), who knows. . . .

Once again, tennis, in its own quiet way, was telling me something that perhaps I should have known. Be aware of your limits. Be kind to your body. Give it everything you've got, but when you have nothing left to give, *schmuck*, you have nothing left to give. Or maybe, the hard way, it was asking me to respect that double dose of reality, those twin pearls of classic wisdom the Oracle at Delphi had already dispensed millennia ago.

Meden agan. Gnothi seauton. (Nothing in excess. Know thyself.)

Apologia for Upchucking

It was common knowledge that before every one of his high school football games, Gerry Rizzuti tossed his cookies.

Gerry was a high-strung halfback at Poly Prep in Brooklyn during the late fifties. He was quick, tricky, and talented. But, strangely, he'll always be remembered (by me, at least) for his pre-game peptic pyrotechnics.

I remember one game in particular. It was in the fall of 1959, and I was sitting in Mr. Desmé's French class, looking out the window (probably during a supremely stimulating lecture on the *passé simple*), when Gerry, juking, feinting, and jitterbugging like a waterbug, runs the opening kickoff down the left sideline ninety-eight yards for a TD. An extraordinary play in itself, but even more so in retrospect, because someone later informed me that Gerry had made the runback a mere fifteen minutes after he'd thrown up all over the locker-room floor.

The reason I am (pardon the expression) bringing this up now is that this memory has stayed with me even today, with important metaphorical ramifications. I think of it every time I get sick to my stomach or am with someone else (particularly a loved one) who does.

It was from that time on, in fact, that I became a confirmed believer in the meliorative impact on the psyche of purging oneself. That is not to say, of course, that willed regurgitation (as in a psychological aberration such as bulimia) is inherently beneficial. But as far as being the body's mechanism for ridding the system of impurities, poisons, even fear and trembling, nothing can beat it. Eat some bad pepperoni? BLECCCCCH: all better! Struggling with a stomach virus? BLECCCCCH: *what* stomach virus? Have that heavy feeling because of the pills you're taking? BLECCCCCH: feel lighter now? Got a bevy of butterflies flapping inside your gut before you go out to talk in front of 500 people? BLECCCCCH: a lepidopterous exeunt!

Since the time of Rizzuti's runback, nearly forty years ago, I've mentioned the event to a bunch of people, as well as my theory of "meliorative barfing" in sports, and in general. And the response is always the same: a rolling of eyes, a condescending pat on the back, a sotto voce remark with the word *disgusting*! embedded somewhere in it. And the discussion has gone no farther. No farther, that is, until thirty-seven years after The Runback, during the quarterfinals of the 1996 U.S. Open.

So there I am, sitting on my couch with a bottle of Pete's Wicked Ale in one hand and a bag of Granny Goose Bavarian pretzels in the other, watching Alex Corretja, one of those Iberian clay-court specialists, in the process of upsetting the heavily-favored and #1-seeded Pete Sampras on his own turf (that is, on his own concrete). It is one of those hot, humid, sticky, windless, disgustingly heavy late-summer dusks for which New York is so famous. And these conditions have probably equalized the match, which under normal circumstances might have been a laugher in favor of the powerful American. But on this eve, the match is excruciatingly close, and it's Sampras, not Corretja, who's struggling. In fact, he's visibly affected by the heat: he looks weak, his head is bowed, he's shaking, he's moving slowly, he's breathing heavily, he's . . . *throwing up!*

Now, normally, the sight of a strong, well-conditioned tennis player in the act of ralphing all over the court will elicit a reaction of surprise and compassion. And indeed, I did experience these feelings toward Sampras, along with enormous admiration for his courage, not a little amazement, and a good degree of empathy. But, funny enough, the main sentiment that was coursing through my body as I watched—in pity and horror and awe—this unbelievable drama unfold right there on center court was . . . *vindication!* At last, my Theory of Meliorative Barfing (TMB) was being tested right there in the Stadium Court at Flushing Meadows in plain view of 18,000 spectators and many, many millions of viewers!

For them, the result of the match at that very moment might have been very much in doubt. After all, Sampras was there tossing his lunch on the court, so it was fair to conclude that he was awfully sick and, at any moment, might not be able to continue. I mean, how much sicker can you get, throwing up there on national television for all to see? Actually, I knew better. The moment the first morsel of sputum was ejected earthward, I knew it was all over. *For the Spaniard!* I knew that Sampras had had the courage to get to this point and to battle through the discomfort and the pain, as sick as he was, but that it was all downhill from here. I knew that now, he had exorcised his microbic demons, his peptic bug, and was essentially purged of the bad guys. Not that he was healed, mind you, but he had to feel at least 1000% better, and, given his superior skills and unparalleled focus, I knew that the match was (pardon the expression) in the bag for Pete. I just knew it. And guess what: it was! Pete (pardon the expression) sucked it up and proceeded to (pardon the expression) wipe the court with Corretja.

For a few moments after the match was over, I just sat there, knowing I had witnessed one of the most courageous performances in Open, if not sports, history. What fortitude! What (pardon the expression) guts! But more than that, my mind wandered back to that day in 1959 and Gerry Rizzuti's runback. Now the two events were finally linked together in perpetuity! But how many similar events had occurred in between that would lend additional credence to my Theory? Who knows? And (probably) who cares? What was important was that I now had closure for my TMB and conclusive proof (on national television, no less) that upchucking—in the locker room, on the tennis court, wherever—was indeed a good thing for the suffering or apprehensive athlete and, under the right circumstances and if used properly and with circumspection, could indeed improve your game.

Latin Trilogy

Anyone who knows me well is aware of the fact that I harbor in my very depths three fundamental and unshakable beliefs. I believe that life is basically good and should be cherished, in some manner or another, each and every day. I believe that as part of this life, sports is a rich and wonderful source of pleasure and joy, a metaphor for existence, a reflection of our noblest (and, for that matter, basest) traits. And I believe that everything started going downhill in this land of ours the minute they eliminated the Latin and Greek requirements from the high school curriculum. So, in an effort to tie together these three beliefs and to underline the appropriateness of applying classical wisdom to athletic experience, I am writing this modest trilogy, hoping it will inspire everyone who loves sports to appreciate its wonder, its agelessness, and the timeless lessons it continually bequeaths us.

I. HOMO FECIT

What—how can I put this delicately?—do these two phenomena have in common: a caveman proudly admiring the very first pile of fecal matter he ever deposited in the woods, and a modern-day baseball player adroitly depositing a perfect sacrifice bunt?

The correct answer is that they are both experiencing one of the oldest instinctive feelings we humans are capable of having: *homo fecit* (or, to translate freely, *look what I did!*). The feeling is ancient, atavistic. (Even God must have chanted the Latin mantra after each of his six back-breaking days of creating stuff.) And it applies to every facet of human existence, at every level, whether we're making a pile of feces or fixing a leak or hooking up a VCR or training a dog or building a sand castle or pruning a bush or completing a crossword puzzle or putting together a swing set or doing a finger painting or conceiving a baby or creating a symphony or writing a book.

In short, *homo fecit* is one of the distinguishing features of the human species. Doing, making, creating, then acknowledging and admiring our accomplishment: this is what truly separates us from the beasts. A loftier way to express the idea is "poetry," from the Greek *poiein*, to do or make or create. But no matter how you say it, it's the uplifting feeling experienced by us humans after we've created something, great or small, that gives us that transcendent, "poetic" satisfaction.

And in what other domain than sports do we more frequently and more intensely experience the feeling of *homo fecit*? (The question is, of course, rhetorical.) Think about it. The wonder of participating in sports is that at virtually every level and at virtually every moment, there is the potential for experiencing some (even small) measure of accomplishment.

Any golfer who's ever teed up his or her ball at a par three knows that if good contact is made and the gods are looking down, a hole-in-one just may occur. And if so, at that moment, the striker of the ball will be filled with the glorious sense that no one else *in the uni-*

verse—not Nicklaus or Watson or Palmer or Player or Trevino or Couples or Irwin or Kite or Crenshaw or Faldo or Price or Norman or even Tiger—could have performed any better at that particular moment. Not only that, but even if you shoot a 95 or a 107 or, for that matter, a 165, there are bound to be at least a few golden moments during the round—a successful escape from a trap, a perfectly-struck shot from an impossible lie, an eight-foot snake of a putt under pressure—that give you the same awesome feeling and the same desire to shout at the top of your lungs: *homo fecit!*

Tennis? Win or lose, it's the same deal. A perfect drop shot? A timely ace? An amazing reflex volley? A topspin lob that lands smack on the baseline? *Homo fecit!*

And so it goes. Whatever sport you participate in, at whatever level and with whatever degree of "success," these moments of doing, making, and creating are there for the taking, seven days a week, twenty-four hours a day! It may take the form of a drag bunt or a shoestring catch or a hook slide or a perfect pivot or working a walk from an oh-and-two count or a jumper from deep in the corner (*swish!*) or a beauty-of-a-bounce-pass or drawing a charge or a great block or a timely interception or a fantastic hip-check or a phenomenal deke or converting a 7–10 split or rolling a turkey or performing an impossible massé or getting two balls on the break or a perfectly placed corner kick or a beautifully timed left cross or an outstanding baton pass or a flawless balance-beam routine or that triple salchow you hit just right. *Homo fecit! Homo fecit!! Homo fecit!!!*

II. Per aspera ad astra

This was one of my favorite Latin *dicta* we had to learn in high school. Yep, we had to memorize a whole slew of these beauties, including the ever-popular *iacta alea est* ("the die is cast"), the always-useful *morituri te salutamus* ("we who are about to die salute you"), and the way-practical *amor omnia vincit* ("love conquers all"). Not to mention other expressions that would prove to be experientially invaluable in life, such as *erat tanta ut non posset moveri etiam par milites* ("she was so large that she could not be moved, even by soldiers"). I can still see ol' Mr. Lucas, staring at us with his stern blue-grey eyes and yelling at us with his raspy voice, attempting to convince us of the sanctity of the classical tradition and the practicality of the Latin language. Good for the vocabulary. Excellent discipline for the mind. (Plus, later, it would help you decipher ivy-league-college mottoes like *in deo speramus, vox clamantis in deserto, veritas, lux et veritas, leges sine moribus vanae*, and, of course, *founded by ezra cornell in 1865*.)

Where was I? Oh yeah: *per aspera ad astra*. Our textbook translated it as "to the stars through bolts and bars." (Today, we would say, "no pain, no gain.") Otherwise stated, the path to heaven isn't always paved with gold. Or, the trip to the promised land ain't no picnic. However you slice it, this is yet another of those insipid clichés that prove themselves time and again, in sports as in life, to be maddeningly true.

Any athlete (as any human) who pretends to understand the scheme of things surely knows one thing: adversity is the great crucible from which all good things are born. Through defeat, victory is that much sweeter; through hard knocks, one becomes stronger, tougher, and above all wiser. No need to press the point: it's so obvious as to not need pressing. But ironically, it's the one point many athletes at every level tend to miss, one point that usually demarcates victory from defeat, and champions from average practitioners.

At the highest level, there's no dearth of images I can evoke (and do, when I find myself staring adversity in the eyes) depicting athletes at their finest, struggling against adversity or the odds or the impossible situation or the uphill battle. I see Bob Baun, coming back just after breaking his right ankle to score the game-winner in overtime of Game 6 of the '64 Stanley Cup finals. I see Shun Fujimoto, exquisite pain etched on his grimacing face, helping Japan beat the U.S.S.R. in the '76 Olympics by landing from the rings on a leg he had broken during the floor exercises. I see Kerry Strug, two decades later, grimacing in much the same situation during her second vault, her ankle sprained and a gold medal on the line. I see Ashley Cooper, bum leg and all, persevering against Mal Anderson in the '58 finals of the U.S. Nationals. I see the hobbling but heroic Willis Reed making his uplifting appearance in the final '73 playoff game to help the Knicks beat the Lakers. I see Kirk Gibson pumping and gimping his way around second after his dramatic homer to win Game 1 of the '88 Series. I see Jackie Joyner-Kersee winning bronze in the long jump with a badly strained hamstring at the '96 Olympics. I see Pete Sampras, regurgitory and gasping with peptic malaise, gutting it out against Alex Corretja in the quarters of the '96 Open. I also see touching images of adversity and struggle in defeat. The photo of Ralph Branca after his Coogan disaster, slumped over in the Bums' locker room and captured touchingly by Barney Stein. And the prostrate Mary Decker, out of the race of her life (the "Zola Budd" race), who would bravely come back years later to reassert herself near the top of the female harriers. And the stunned Bill Buckner, reacting to Mookie's squibber after letting it go through the wickets in that exquisitely vital '86 Series moment, who would hold his head high right up to his retirement from the sport in which he excelled. And Dan Jansen, odds-on favorite felled like a tree by the pressures of his life and the moment, who would courageously return to the Games and satisfy the skating expectations the whole world had of him. And the bloodied but unbowed Y.A. Tittle doubled over on the sidelines after a loss to the '64 Steelers in his final year of competition (and unforgettably snapped by Morris Berman). And, of course, the stunned Greg Norman, after giving away the '96 Open to Faldo, who would take the bitter defeat like a man and maintain his #1 world ranking.

And any little kids I've ever seen in a playground or a field or a schoolyard or a driveway or a rink or at a driving range or on a track or opposite a backboard, staying for hours, solitary, long after they should've left, practicing, practicing, until their knuckles are bleeding and their bones are sore and their clothes are completely soaked with the sweat of their efforts. And all of whom know, surely as well as the most celebrated pro athletes, that the path to the stars is indeed paved with asperity.

III. VIRTUS VICTRIX FORTUNAE

This was the Latin motto of Poly Prep, my high school. It means something like "character is the conqueror of fate" or "character conquers chance." It really doesn't translate exactly into English, but you get the picture. Well, as often happens regarding something that's always there right under your nose day after day, I never really thought about the motto when I was in school. Just sort of took it for granted as it sat there on the ol' seal.

I've often thought of it since, though, particularly through the prism of my athletic experiences. For me, it really has to do with the burning issue of "luck" in sports. So let's get it clear from the git-go: when you get right down to it, there is no such thing as luck in sports.

Oh sure, how many times do we hear winners giving post-game or post-match interviews who, when asked how they came to win, reply that they were "lucky" or "fortunate" or "got the breaks" on that day.

Fiddlesticks.

What they meant to say is that they were good and that they're also modest. Truth is, the ball is always going to bounce one way or the other, and there's no controlling it. I'd venture to say that if you counted up all the "lucky" bounces and all the "funny" bounces you ever got in your athletic career, you'd just about break even.

There's an old saw in sports that goes, "I'd rather be lucky than good."

Hogwash.

As I mentioned, the bounces even out. But next time you find yourself watching (or playing in) a really tense situation—a third-set tiebreak or a ninth-inning duel or a final possession requiring a buzzer-beater or a meaningful four-foot putt or a fourth-and-three with the game on the line—try to notice who comes out on top and why. Sure, there may be many reasons for the outcome (it's *not* luck!), but I'd venture to say that the player who's aggressive in the clutch will generally win. The one who goes for it, who plays the situation instead of letting it play him, who has a game plan and follows it strictly instead of waiting for "something to happen," who doesn't hold back or play defensively generally has the psychological edge: inside, he knows he's giving it everything he's got; and from his opponent's viewpoint, it's generally more intimidating to see the other guy being aggressive than seeing him play wait-and-see. In my experience, taking the bull by the horns works a lot more than not.

In the end, it all comes down to character. Who believes in himself more? Who is strong enough to force the issue? Who is focused enough to block out distractions and concentrate on the moment? Who will let it all hang out and thus take risks that will pay dividends? Or, in three wonderfully pithy words, *virtus victrix fortunae.*

Perhaps Branch Rickey expressed it even more powerfully: *Luck is the residue of design.* (If you work hard and try hard and have a consistent game plan, then good things will happen.)

Or maybe it was Tina Turner: *What's luck got to do with it?*

The Biggest Drum in the World

It was the spring of 1972, and I had just accepted a job at Purdue University. I was teaching at Harvard, but this was a chance to get on a tenure-track and to earn some "real" money. Now, prior to this, I had known only two facts about Indiana: 1. Herb Shriner came from there; and 2. this state was colored yellow (a fact I had picked up from playing "Game of the States" as a kid). So, that summer, my then–wife and eleven-month-old son Noah flew to the Hoosier state, and I drove from Cambridge with my (appropriately!) yellow lab, Barnaby. It would be the first time I'd be living west of Brooklyn, and frankly, I was a bit apprehensive.

The trip there was uneventful, except for the vibrating bed Barnaby and I enjoyed at the Holiday Inn in Sharon, Pennsylvania, after nine grueling hours on the road (I did most of the driving).

West Lafayette, Indiana, is a sleepy little college town situated in the northern half of the state, not terribly far from the sleepy little towns of Kokomo and Peru. (That's about as exotic as Indiana gets.) The campus was not remarkable in any way I could make out, except

169

for the fact that there appeared to be no tall buildings on it. Not surprising if you've ever traveled through the rest of the state. But subsequently, I learned the real reason for this phenomenon: Purdue was originally a land-grant college, and its founder, John Purdue, was an acrophobic who had decreed in the by-laws that no building over four stories ever be built on campus. Whatever.

Finding stimulating things to do on campus was a challenge, at least for someone used to big cities and just having lived in Cambridge, Mass. (The first inkling I had that things might be different was the compound name of the local newspaper in Lafayette: not the *Times* or the *Post* or even the *Herald*, but the *Journal and Courier*.) In fact, there are only two "events" I have retained in my memory to this day from the two years I spent there. The first was a tornado (the first I had seen since the one that whisked Dorothy and Toto to Oz, and to this day, the only one I've ever seen in person) that came within a mile of our rented house at 307 Russell St., a few blocks from campus. The second was the sight and smell of a suckling pig some guys in the fraternity house across the street were preparing in a pit one sultry evening (the most alarming, traumatic exemplar of culture shock a New York Jew could possibly experience).

In the West Lafayette of 1972, there was very little in the way of theater or movies or bookstores or cafés. Plus the Chinese restaurants in the area (both of them) sucked. Which brings us, of course, to sports (*aha!*) as a source of diversionary satisfaction. From the viewpoint of a participant, the pickin's were mighty slim. For one thing, no one had even heard of squash (actually, they *had*, but only as a vegetable): if you wanted to play, you had to hop a plane to the nearest court, which happened to be in Toronto. There were also no indoor tennis courts, so much of the time (if you could find any decent players), you had to play in conditions that were either unbearable (40 degrees below and windy) or unbearable (120 degrees above and humid). Golf? The only way you can design a course is, naturally, if you have hills. (Indiana's flatness makes Florida's look like the Himalayas.)

If you were content to spectate, the pickin's were somewhat less slim. But barely. On the professional level, things were pretty grim. There weren't many TV sports stations available, and the few you could tune into were in Chicago (e.g., WLS). Which meant the best you could do was to watch the Cubs do their best to not win another pennant. Or suffer with the Bears-between-Sayers-and-Payton or commiserate with the way-before-MJ-Bulls (led by Norm Van Lier).

At the college level, as luck would have it, I just barely missed being at Purdue to witness their greatest football player ever (Leroy Keyes) and their greatest basketball player ever (Rick Mount). Keyes was a powerful runner who came in third in the Heisman voting in '67 and second (to O.J.) in '68. Mount was one of the purest shooters I'd ever seen and even today, I'd rank his jumper (along with Jerry West's) as the purest shot in the history of roundball. But alas, while I was there, neither of them was; so neither team had a "star," and both struggled.

Despite these arid athletic conditions in West Lafayette, there *was* in fact an oasis in the desert, one single object worthy of my sporting admiration that has stuck in my mind after lo these many years.

The Drum.

You see, as a last resort, I used to take Noah to Purdue's mid-week football practices. He was barely a year old, and I suppose I was attempting, in some feeble paternal way, to inculcate in him (in a purely osmotic way, of course) a love of sports. As he watched these huge brutes practice, I reasoned, a love of competition (in addition to that available to him through his paternal DNA) might somehow rub off. The first time we watched practice together, however, I realized at one point that we weren't in fact watching practice together. While I was witnessing all the blocking and tackling and running and passing and catching and strategizing, my infant son had his eyes glued to one object the entire time. An object that had nothing to do with the game of football per se. It was a drum, a big drum, a very big drum. In fact, this drum was so big, it looked like it could be the biggest drum in the world. And when I finally transferred my gaze from the players to the object of Noah's desire and got a closer look, I realized that it *was* the biggest drum in the world. How did I know? Because written on the drum, in big, bold, fancy letters, was the following message:

THE BIGGEST DRUM IN THE WORLD.

And every time we'd go to practice, we'd basically end up admiring the size of this humongous percussive behemoth, watching it go back and forth, pushed by members of the marching band in anticipation of a half-time extravaganza the following Saturday afternoon. Boy, was it big! I mean, it was so big that I'm sure Noah, who couldn't read at the time, somehow sensed that this was without a doubt the biggest drum in the world.

Yessirree Bob, besides the tornado and the roasting of that suckling pig, the biggest drum in the world remains, to this very day, the only memory I have retained from my twenty-four months spent in West Lafayette. A testimony to the power of advertising perhaps. (I *still* know, more than a quarter of a century later, where the world's biggest drum is located!) But if you're expecting some dramatic, symbolic ending to this story, you'd be sorely mistaken. Like Noah's growing up to become a world-famous drummer or an NFL star. Nope, as it turns out, today he's a third-degree black belt in karate and is hoping to have a career in film directing, neither of which has anything at all to do with the drum.

What you *can* take away from this tale, however, is a bit of invaluable sports trivia that you might want to add to that mountain of relatively useless athletic information being stored presently inside your hippocampus. So if any of your cronies gets into a hot-and-heavy trivia match with you, just whip out this baffling, tasty little tidbit ("Where's the biggest drum in the world located?") to shut him up. And if, on his thirtieth try, he throws up his arms in desperation and wildly guesses *"Peru?"* you can grin wickedly at him and answer, "No, but you're getting *very* close!"

You Can Leave Your Hat On

First, a tip of the cap. To "the one and only" Joe Cocker. Definitely (along with James Taylor and Carole King and Paul McCartney and John Lennon and Phil Collins and Elton John and Paul Simon and Georges Brassens and Jacques Brel and Francesco DeGregori and Emily Saliers) my favorite singer/songwriter of all time. His trademark song (written by Randy Newman, who, now that I think about it, also belongs in my pantheon) has become a cheeky little number entitled "You Can Leave Your Hat On," which goes something like this (actually, it goes *exactly* like this):

Baby take off your coat,
Real slow . . .
Take off your shoes,
Ah take off your shoes baby . . .
Take off your dress,
Yes yes yes . . .
But you can leave your hat on,
You can leave your hat on,
You can leave your hat on . . .

Well, sir, I'm listening to his wonderful new CD ("Organic"), and cut #12 just happens to be the "hat song" whose immortal lyrics you've just hummed silently. And I start thinking about those lyrics, ·as is my wont, in the context of sports. And whaddya know? An idea for an essay pops into my head: *just like that!* (I'm always startled and bemused by the mysterious way in which poetic inspiration slithers its way into one's consciousness.)

So I'm pondering the issue of hats in sports, and the first thing I think about when the chorus comes around (*you can leave your hat on*) is how very special Willie Mays was as an athlete. I mean, baseball is a game where everyone wears a hat, right? And every hat is basically the same (a cap with a peak), differing, one from another, only by team logo and color. Part of that whole "uniform" thing. And you *can* leave your hat on; in fact, motivated by tradition and propriety and team cohesiveness, you're pretty much *obliged* to leave it on at all times. And in the history of the game, which goes back about a century and a half, only one player *couldn't* leave his hat on: Willie! He played with such gleeful abandon, of course, that his cap-flying-off-as-he-slid became one of the trademarks that set him apart from all the rest.

Then I start thinking about the hats worn in different sports. Naturally, I ruminate, the more contact there happens to exist in a given sport, the less chance a hat is worn. (Instead, they're replaced by helmets.) Which means that golf, where the least contact occurs, should have the most interesting hats. Which it does! Of course, in the old days most everybody wore one; then there was a lull, after Hogan and Snead (both of whom had their trademark hats), where only a few golfers wore one; and now, for whatever reason, there seems to be a glorious renaissance in haberdashery. There are, in fact, hats all over the pro golf tours. Many of the women wear assorted caps and hats and visors, but special mention should go, of course, to the always spiffily-coiffed Michelle McGann. After all these years, Chi

Chi's still wearing that funky little brimmed one, and Bob Murphy has his own trademark turned-up, wide-brimmed plantation hat. And Greg Norman has made the white (or black) hat with the shark-logo band quite stylish. And Tom Kite's been wearing his wide-brimmed straw job for quite a while now. And I love Payne Stewart's winsome little quasi-beret cap. And how about Jesper Parnevik's "backwards" look? And suddenly, nearly everyone and his caddie seems to be wearing a cap: Tom Watson's Ram cap, Tom Lehman's Dockers cap, Tiger Woods' Nike cap, Duffy Waldorf's funkily-splattered cap, Jack Nicklaus' Golden Bear cap. Giving each golfer a much-needed personal signature to their persona (since they wear neither uniforms nor numbers). Not that you wouldn't recognize a Watson or a Woods or a Nicklaus by their inimitable swings, but the hat's a nice touch, dontcha think? Only thing I wonder about is why many of the Europeans haven't gotten with the program. I mean, why doesn't Faldo ever wear a hat? Or Montgomerie? Or Langer? Or Olazabal or Ballesteros? Maybe their Continental "dos" are too classy to be messed up?

Contact-wise, next comes tennis. Same pattern as in golf: in the old days, plenty of players covered their heads with hats of one kind or another. Dr. James Dwight (the "George Washington" of American tennis) wore an old-style baseball cap, Aussie Norman Brookes wore a stylish floppy cap, one of the Four Musketeers (Jean Borotra) wore a blue beret and another (René Lacoste) wore a floppy cap. Then there was a long hat-wearing draught, interrupted only by extreme heat, which forced many of the Aussies in the fifties and sixties to wear those floppy Aussie "bonnets." (Dick Savitt also wore one in the '51 Davis Cup tie against Japan, and so did Stan Smith on occasion.) One of the few exceptions, of course, was Frew McMillan, the stylish South African doubles player who always wore a "Ben Hogan" hat when he played singles, or doubles with the balding (and hatless) Bob Hewitt. Nowadays, heat (and perhaps the scare of skin cancer?) has taken its toll, and darn near everyone's wearing a cap again. I think it's great, and it's done a lot to individualize the players and make the game more colorful. There's even a bunch of players (Marc Goellner of Germany and Goran Ivanisevic of Croatia, to name two) wearing them backwards, home-boy style.

Baseball we've already discussed (Willie vs. the rest). But I forgot to mention the innovative '80s N.Y. Mets' "rally caps" (backwards, inside-out), which set a glorious trend still practiced today. (Boys *will* be boys. . . .)

Speaking of individualization (after all, the prime function of the sporting hat or cap or helmet), why don't pro football players put the same designs on their helmets as college players do? I sort of like those buckeye leaves or tiger paws or whatever: you know, the decals they put up there when they make a big tackle or a touchdown or a long reception. You think it's a question of not wanting to manifest any excess ego? *Right!* And all the other sports where you wear a helmet (cycling, skiing, ski jumping, hockey, etc.) could surely follow suit.

And why don't basketball players wear caps, huh? It'd be neat: they wear hats in virtually every other sport, so why not hoops? You could charge special fouls for knocking a guy's cap off. (No arbitrariness here: it's either on his head or off!) You'd have to wear the cap backwards, of course, as the brim might get in the way of your stroke. Just an idea. . . .

I just think hats are cool. And as long as I'm up here on my soapbox, why don't they wear them in *every* sport? There'd be these cool Panamas for bowlers and sporty bowlers for billiard players, and skimmers and Easter-bonnet deals for those men and women who run around with the dogs at those dog shows. And archers could wear those felt Robin-Hood caps with the feathers. And riflers could wear Aaron-Burr beanies or something. And the folks who play soccer and track and field and gymnastics could take the lead from beach-volleyball players, who all look so cool, especially the greatest of them all, Karch Kiraly, with his backwards pink Speedo cap. Yep: athletes of all shapes and sizes in all sports, *you can leave your hat on!*

I've saved for last the absolutely coolest sports hat of all time: Ivan Lendl's French-foreign-legion hat—you know, the one with that flap in the back he used to wear to protect his neck when it was 108 degrees? As a competitor, Lendl had lots of guts to begin with, but I think it took an extra portion of them to come out in front of all those people and actually wear that bizarre-looking baby. But I'll tell you, as laughable as it looked, it sure did the job, keeping him far more protected from the sun than any of his long-suffering (hatless and neck-exposed) opponents. Which, as it happens, brings to mind another song, one I used to sing all the time as a kid:

> *I eat my peas with honey,*
> *I've done it all my life;*
> *It sure tastes kind of funny,*
> *But it keeps them on the knife.*

Dollar Nassau

For the past forty years (give or take), my father and I have had a running golf game of Dollar Nassau. And for about thirty-five of those years, I was busy redefining the expression, " 'Tis better to give than to receive." (For those of you sheltered souls who aren't acquainted with the rules, they're simple: match play, whoever wins the front nine gets a buck, whoever wins the back nine gets a buck, and whoever wins the eighteen gets a buck; so, you can win three bucks or two bucks or a buck or break even or lose three bucks or two bucks or a buck.)

Here's the brief history behind our game. My Dad taught me how to play golf at the age of twelve (he was forty-four). He taught me the basic shots, including all the delicate ones around the green, and how to play uphill, downhill, and sidehill lies. He taught me how to remember every shot on every hole. (His memory is legend: he was once playing a "Phillies" match—very complicated scoring—with three other physicians, and on the fourteenth hole, the wind blows away the scorecard. And he doesn't even bother to chase it because he remembers *every* shot *everyone* has taken on *every* hole!) He also tried to teach me patience (including how to wait nicely on the tee while Bermudaed old men were up ahead of you taking *hours* to line up their putts and do their waggles) and sacrifice (why it makes sense to pitch out of the rough, as opposed to threading the ball through two huge spruces), although it took me years—even decades!—to have even an inkling of what he was getting at. (I also got a little help from Ellsworth Vines—then the club pro—who, with Althea Gibson, was the greatest combination tennis/golf phenomenon in the history of the two sports.) It all happened at Inwood Country Club, on Long Island Sound (and, ironically, in *Nassau* County). A honey of a golf course, where they played the 1923 U.S. Open won by Bobby Jones in a celebrated playoff and which, on a really windy day, was a real sonuvabitch to play.

Inwood is still today a very special golf course: to my knowledge, it's the only top-level course in the world with three consecutive par fives (holes 3–5), which in itself is remarkable, to say nothing of the fact that they're followed by two consecutive par threes. So, after I'm able to play a round of golf without embarrassing myself too much (and being the competitive youngster that I was), I insist on playing Dollar Nassaus with Dad whenever we get the chance. Now first, let me describe my father's golf game, to give you an idea of what I'm up against, of the mountain I have to climb every time we tee it up. He was the kind of golfer that any club player (however good) would have nightmares about playing. He wasn't a very long hitter, but his short game was murder (I mean *murder!*). He was, in those days, about a twelve or thirteen handicap, which meant that, however good you were, he would always (I mean *always!*) beat the crap out of you (we're talking *grosses* of golf balls). In our matches, the usual scenario would be that I'd outdrive him by about sixty yards, then little by little the ol' fox would sneak up on me (I'd usually be deep in the rough, he in the fairway), and by the time we'd get to the green—*presto!*—we'd be even. Then, he'd invariably hole *his* putt while I'd miss mine (even though, great sportsman that he was, he'd always help me read it), and I'd walk off the green feeling more macho and more manly and more powerful than he but having lost the goddam hole! And this same scenario wouldn't happen just occasionally: it would be the rule to which exceptions occurred only (or so it seemed) by accident.

To refresh your memory, the unique front nine went like this: 4-4-5-5-5-3-3-4-4 (par 37). The back nine was a more conventional 3-4-4-4-3-5-4-4-4 (par 35). To this day (forty years after I first played the course), I can still remember nearly every blade of grass, every bunker, every tree that came between my four irons and the green. Basically, it's a course designed for the experienced, mature, masochistic golfer, with all that wind coming off the Sound and lots of trouble (marshes, water, deep rough, out-of-bounds, *many* tall trees). Dad and I must have played over a hundred Dollar Nassaus through the years at Inwood. And the combination of his flawless short game and my youthful exuberance (read: impatience) and too-bold play conspired to prevent me—no matter how well I played—from ever winning a *single* piece of paper with George Washington's picture on the front of it. Oh, once—I think it was one of the final times we played the course, and some of Dad's lessons of patience and sacrifice finally began to sink in—I finally halved the back nine and lost only two bucks. Talk about Pyrrhic victories! Maybe it was a barely legible scrawl, but was it finally the very first hint of writing on the wall? A watershed tie? A harbinger of things to come?

I'll fast-forward, not wishing to burden you with all the gory details of our subsequent matches at various courses. Suffice it to say that my folks eventually moved to Florida, where they live essentially *on* a golf course (The Golf and Racquet Club at Eastpointe, in Palm Beach Gardens). And whenever I got my butt down to that part of the country, Dad and I would, of course, play our traditional Dollar Nassau. The new course wasn't the monster Inwood was—with wide, forgiving fairways and much less trouble—and I was older and wiser and Dad was older and, shall we say, less erect. And guess what. Yep: same result! Every time we play, he's wending his way down the fairway and I'm crushing my drive and walking light-years ahead of him, and we both get around the green in two (or three) strokes, and he's up and in, and I'm up and around and in *and down one*. And it's so damn maddening, I could toss my clubs in the lake and make Tommy Bolt proud. But Dad has taught me well: I am patient and well-behaved and grit my teeth. And I wait and wait and wait . . . until *that glorious day* finally comes!

So this one fine morning, I'm playing out of my mind, hitting every ball on the screws and even making some long putts, and whad-dya know? *I beat him three ways!* Now clearly, Dad isn't the golfer he used to be, especially around the greens, but what the hell? The three crisp dollar bills I always bring with me will, for once, *remain in my pocket*! And—*mirabile dictu!*—Dad smiles graciously and hands me three of *his* bucks, and it's as if I'd just won the friggin' lottery!

What else can I say? When I get home (to California), I immedi-ately pin the three bucks on the wall near my nighttable as a reminder of my long-awaited victory. But wait! That's not the end of the story, not (pardon the expression) by a long shot. So I wake up in a cold sweat at about 3 A.M. one morning a few weeks after my stir-ring victory and I'm thinking that I'm getting all excited about final-ly winning a match I've been trying to win for thirty-four years and what *really* happened is that golf, that great teacher, is having (as it always does) the last word and what I've actually "accomplished" is beating someone who's nearly eighty and who's not the same chipper and putter he used to be and it's something I could never do when he was at his best and in his prime and at the height of his powers but now I've done it when he's not at his best and what's the big deal? Ah, hubris and false pride! Ah, the self-delusion of youth! Had I forgotten to heed the most important lesson of all my father taught me years ago? *Never let golf go to your head: the next shot may bite you in the ass.*

Priests
of the
Invisible

I taught the concept of poetry for over twenty years of my life. It's a difficult one to teach (let alone to understand), but one of the best definitions I ever came across was formulated by the incomparable Wallace Stevens: *The poet is the priest of the invisible.* What follows is a discussion of how this concept relates to athletes; ultimately, it is paying homage to those athletes—those very, very rare athletes—whom I consider to be true poets.

So what is poetry anyway? Simply put, it's the very special use of words that creates a special world transforming and transcending the one we know. It's the creation of a level of feeling and knowing and perception that we've never before felt or known or imagined. It's starting with a blank piece of paper and—*poof!*—filling it with the magic of images and rhythms. It's the uncovering of what is not visible or obvious in everyday reality, and the discovering of new ways of seeing the world and all its silences, mysteries, and paradoxes. It's all this and much more. In essence, we don't really understand how a poet creates this very special universe; all we can do is attempt to understand and appreciate the magic sitting right there on the page. For me, it's a rare and ineffable feeling I've experienced from time to time, particularly in the arts: stepping into Amiens cathedral or Le Corbusier's church of Notre-Dame-du-Haut at Ronchamp; visiting the Rodin museum in Paris or the Picasso museum in Barcelona or the Prado (of Goya and Bosch) in Madrid or the Rembrandt Huis in Amsterdam or the Egyptian exhibit in the British Museum or the Sistine ceiling; reading Lao-tzu or Shakespeare or Dostoevsky or Poe or Mallarmé or Rilke; listening to Bach's *Goldberg Variations* or anything Mozart ever wrote or Beethoven's Ninth or the songs of Gilbert and Sullivan or Georges Brassens or John Lennon.

And so it is with the poet/athlete: we don't really understand how the magic is created, how the invisible possibility becomes realized with the wave of a hand (or a bat or a club or a racquet). Is it a question of physical talent (speed, strength, reflexes)? Or mental agility? Or good decision-making? Or maybe a combination of all of these? My hunch is that it comes down to instinct and intuition, qualities shared by all athletes, to be sure, but exquisitely refined in only a few chosen ones. We may not understand their magic, but we can appreciate and enjoy it. We can sit there in the stands or in front of the TV set and be awe-inspired: the mouth opens, the jaw drops. . . .

In my lifetime, I have seen only five "priests of the invisible" creating their poetry in the game of baseball. Five. Now let's get one thing straight: I've seen my fair share of absolutely *wonderful* players: great hitters, amazing fielders, phenomenal pitchers. For the record, my favorites: Ted Williams, Stan Musial, Mickey Mantle, Al Kaline, Don Mueller (yes, Don Mueller!), Ernie Banks, Rod Carew, George Brett, Wade Boggs, Pete Rose, Willie McCovey, Reggie Jackson, Hank Aaron, Mike Schmidt, Ken Griffey, Jr., Barry Bonds; Ozzie Smith, Brooks Robinson, Luis Aparicio, Gil Hodges, Keith Hernandez, Don Mattingly, Vic Power, Carl Furillo, Bobby Shantz,

Jim Kaat; Satchel Paige, Bob Feller, Sal Maglie, Robin Roberts, Warren Spahn, Whitey Ford, Bob Gibson, Juan Marichal, Hoyt Wilhelm, Don Drysdale, Jim Palmer, Steve Carlton, Tom Seaver, Nolan Ryan, Greg Maddux. All greats, but now let's talk *poetry*.

O.K., here are my five picks. Willie Mays. Jackie Robinson. Roberto Clemente. Sandy Koufax. Minnie Minoso. Now mind you, these are extremely subjective choices. But every time these guys would do something—almost *anything!*—I would get this strange feeling. (Or, to steal a metaphor the great Art Director Seymon Ostilly would use when, as a creative advertising team, we would come upon an exciting idea: *my nipples would get hard*.) I mean, these guys could create poetry out of nothing, whether making a basket catch and throwing a guy out at home in virtually the same motion or driving a pitcher crazy by jitterbugging off third or lashing a pitch that was two feet out of the strike zone to right field with the flick of the wrists or being absolutely, embarrassingly unhittable or sliding home with rage and flair at the age of fifty. They just *had it*, period.

In basketball, of all the great ones I've had the privilege to see, I'd have to say there were eight who separated themselves from the mere mortals playing on the same court. (Not that players like Schayes, Pettit, The Hawk, Baylor, Barry, West, Russ, Wilt, Kareem, and Walton weren't great. But my choices were, well, *poets*.) The Magnificent Eight: The Big O, Dr. J., The Pearl, Larry, Magic, Michael, and my two favorites of all time, Cooz and Pistol. I think these last two were so special to me because of two "poetic" qualities that always fascinated me: instinct and creativity. They just *knew* where everyone was on the court, and they'd improvise stuff that you couldn't *imagine* someone could make up. Their peripheral vision was so refined that I've always had a hunch there was a chameleon or two in their genealogy. And besides being wonderful players, they were arguably the two greatest entertainers we've ever seen at the pro level.

In football, there were six players who, every time they touched the ball, anything could happen. (Hey! That's *anacoluthon*!) Jim Brown. Willie Galimore. Johnny Rodgers. O. J. Simpson. Barry Sanders. And my favorite of all time, Gale Sayers. Their instincts were so powerful (translated into "happy feet" and jukes that could create not only poetry, but groin pulls in the most competent of defensive linesmen) that they were somehow able to appear effortless (as all great artists do) in their almost lyrical circumvention of opposing players. I never saw a back go through people like Brown or around people like Galimore or Sayers; explode through the line more, well, explosively than O.J.; juke and feint more eloquently than Rodgers or Sanders. But Sayers was, for me, the most poetic of all these grid-iron priests. Before the age of true specialization, he was the rare genius who could be truly dominant as both running back and kick-returner.

Hockey's easy. There's Orr (*by far*, the most explosive defensive scorer and skater ever) and Lemieux (the second most explosive offensive scorer ever). And then, way above the rest, there's The Great One. What's so "poetic" about Gretzky is that even at a ripe old age (he's a Ranger now, and I can finally root for his team!), he has a sixth sense about him. He's the only NHL player I've ever had fun watching *without the puck*! You can just watch him behind the net, cruising, waiting for the opportunity, and then, out of thin air, he finds someone open. It isn't so much that he's a great skater (in fact, there was none better), but that he has an uncanny ability to see plays develop that no one else on the ice (especially defensemen!) can. In a nutshell, he can see what's invisible and consistently transform it into reality, in the form of an assist or a goal.

Of all the great tennis players I've seen, Gonzalez was the most dominant (and maybe the best), Connors the fiercest fighter, Hoad and Sampras the strongest, Rosewall the most durable, and Borg the most focused. They were all *great*, mind you, but, in my mind, the three "priests of the invisible" were Nastase, Laver, and McEnroe. I think that, like my baseball choices, it had a lot to do with their hands. Nastase used a very small grip and was somehow able to manufacture shots with a flick of the wrists and great racquet control: a true master of creative shot-making and the unexpected. Laver's left arm was nearly twice the size of his right: with this sledgehammer, he had terrific strength. A big part of his dominant game was also the creativity he had when it came to spinning the ball, and that he did with his quick wrists. But the best part of this poet's game was between his ears: he always seemed to know which shot to hit, and when, and where. Among the three, I'd choose McEnroe as the most lyrical and spontaneous poet. A lot of it was in his soft hands (actually, "hand": his left one!). Like Nastase, he used the racquet like a sort of magic wand and could virtually steer the ball exactly where he wanted to with the softness and deftness of his left hand. Making him the greatest volleyer and doubles player ever.

Which leaves golf. Now, I'm not talking about machines. The greatest golfing machine, by far, was Nicklaus. Among active players, Faldo is a distant second. And I always love watching Watson, Palmer, Miller, and Couples, all of whom have as much talent as anyone around. But for me, there are only two *poets*: Lee Trevino and Chi Chi Rodriguez. Again, it's in the hands. Trevino can do *anything* with his hands: make the ball go right or left, invent ways to get out of tough situations, use his hands to spin the ball, to make it fade, draw, hook, slice, die, whatever. (I also like the way he plays so quickly, which is what I also liked so much about Watson and Julius Boros.) And Chi Chi: *forget it!* I once saw him in a shot-making competition, and I couldn't believe my eyes! The guy has magical hands, that's all there is to it. I don't care what situation he's in out there on the course: behind a mole-hill, say, under a Coke bottle, with his back-swing obstructed. He'd take a putter with his left hand and hit it 60 degrees, with backspin, and slide it under the Coke bottle, through the mole-hill (leaving the sleeping mole undisturbed!), popping the ball onto the green, where it would spin back to within an inch of the cup. I mean, he could put any kind of spin on the ball, do whatever the conditions or the situation warranted. He's the most creative ball-striker I've ever seen. (And, like Lee and Julius and Tom, he also plays wonderfully quickly.)

So there ya have it. Willie, Jackie, Roberto, Sandy, Minnie, The Big O, Dr. J., The Pearl, Larry, Magic, Michael, Cooz, Pistol, Brown, Galimore, Rodgers, Simpson, Sanders, Sayers, Orr, Lemieux, Gretzky, Nastase, Laver, McEnroe, Trevino, Chi Chi.

Priests of the invisible, all!

American Chattah

C'mon, baby, you can do it,
* you can do it, you can do it!*
Let's go, kiddo, show 'em watcha got!
Chuck it in, chuck it in good,
* chuck it, chuck it, chuck it!*
Hey, babe, one mo,' one mo,' jes' one mo'!
Hey, battah battah, hey battah battah. . . . SWING battah!
C'mon, honey, make him hit, make him hit!
Here we go, baby, here we go, here we go!
O.K., kiddo, hit the corner, hit the corner, hit the corner!
C'mon, pitchah, c'mon, pitchah, pitchah, pitchah!
Let's go, one mo' time, one mo' time, one mo' time!
OK, you know what to do, you know what to do!

Let any human being who hasn't spent time in America (or any American who's lived in an incubator all his life) read the above, and he'll surely regard it as nonsensical, cacophonous gobbledygook. Because nowhere else on the face of the planet, besides on a kid's baseball field somewhere in this great country of ours, can this hypnotizing chant of diamond "chattah," this secret code of cowhide solidarity be deemed intelligible.

What I find so fascinating about Yankee adolescent baseball lingo, from a purely *linguistic* standpoint, is its utterly charming symbolic and atavistic nature. It's a wonderful example of a combination of words with perfectly acceptable grammar and syntax that has absolutely no semantic content, no discernible meaning in the real world. A series of expressions that ostensibly communicates ideas, but that, code-like, instead communicates something way beyond its denotative, superficial meaning.

What chattah does, at a very basic level, is create *rhythm* by the simple use of repetition. It almost doesn't matter what the repeated words are (as it happens, they have to do with the pitcher's potential efficacity, but for all intents and purposes, they could espouse any mantric object). Anyway, what this dizzying rhythm creates is a feeling, a feeling communicated to many people and at many levels. (Pretty good for a bunch of meaningless words, huh?) First, it communicates a feeling of solidarity between the chatterer and the pitcher. Next, it communicates a sense of well-being to the chatterer him(or her)self, a sort of external monologue that gives moral support to the chatterer just as much as to the object of his (or her) gobbledygook. Then, like an infectious laugh, it affects first one teammate of the chatterer, then another, then another, creating a snowball effect of well-being and comfort. Finally, when it has permeated everyone on the field, it reaches the level of the "team-in-itself" (apologies to Kant). So that as a result of this innocent, rhythmic babble, not only does the pitcher feel buoyed, but so do chatterer and entire ball club alike, all now magically energized into performing at their best. And all because of a series of seemingly hollow, meaningless, nonsensical, redundant clumps of semantically poppycockish Jabberwocky!

Only in America.

The Thirty Lessons of Sports

Actually, there are probably many hundreds, if not thousands, of lessons to be learned from sports, if you believe (as I do) that sports is truly a metaphor for life. But thirty is a nice, workable number; so in this spirit, I hereby offer you my top thirty lessons. (After each one, in parentheses, are helpful illustrative sporting examples culled from my cerebral file of basically useless information.)

O.K., here goes:

1. *Hey, ya never know.* (Texas Western beats Kentucky, '66 NCAA finals)
2. *Winning and losing are impostors: just try your best.* (Ralph Branca's life after 10/3/51)
3. *Never, ever underestimate your opponent.* (Liston loses to Clay; the hare loses to the tortoise)
4. *Never, ever overestimate your opponent.* (Fleck beats Hogan in '55 U.S. Open playoff)

5. *Put together the best athletes, and you don't necessarily have the best team.* (any playoff series in the '60s between the Celts and the Lakers)

6. *A good defense usually beats a good offense.* (any playoff series in the '60s between the Celts and the Lakers)

7. *Fame is fleeting.* (the baseball careers of Karl Spooner and Bob Lennon)

8. *There is no justice.* (the baseball careers of Harry Agganis and Herb Score)

9. *Never, ever give up.* (Gonzalez beats Pasarell, first round '69 Wimbledon, 22–24, 1–6, 16–14, 6–3, 11–9)

10. *Patience is a virtue.* (hopefully, any Red Sox or Cubs fan)

11. *Don't overthink things.* (anyone who's ever addressed a golf ball)

12. *Ya gotta believe!* ('69 Mets, '69 Jets, '80 U.S. Olympic hockey squad)

13. *Ya gotta have heart.* (the Washington Senators of "Damn Yankees" fame, Bob Baun, Shun Fujimoto, Willis Reed, Kerry Strug, Ashley Cooper, Kirk Gibson, Jackie Joyner-Kersee, Pete Sampras)

14. *Master the fundamentals.* (anyone who ever played for Red Auerbach, John Wooden, or Vince Lombardi)

15. *Nobody's perfect.* (exception: Don Larsen)

16. *Ya can't win 'em all.* (Roy Face's '59 season)

17. *Always respect your opponent.* (C.K. Yang and Rafer Johnson; any Aussie tennis player)

18. *It's not how you look, it's how you play the game.* (Miller Barber, Pancho Segura, Ewell Blackwell, Earl Monroe, Lou Campi)

19. *Humility builds character.* (Bill Buckner, Dan Jansen, Ralph Branca, Mary Decker, Greg Norman, anyone who's ever rooted for the Red Sox or the Cubs, anyone who's ever played golf)

20. *Drive for show, putt for dough.* (anyone who's ever played golf)

21. *The bigger they are, the harder they fall.* (Clay beats Liston twice, Jimmy Connors' service return)

22. *Grace under pressure makes a winner.* (Jackie Robinson's entire career; the NCAA shots of Keith Smart, Magic Johnson, and Christian Laettner in the final seconds; any "two-minute drill" of Unitas, Elway, or Montana; any Aussie tennis champ)

23. *Pay attention to the details.* (the mental lapses of Fred Merkle, Roberto de Vicenzo, and Chris Webber)

24. *Enjoy!* (the attitudes of Willie Mays, Ernie Banks, Magic Johnson, Lee Trevino, Chi Chi Rodriguez, and Jimmy Connors)

25. *Respect tradition.* (the attitudes of Pete Sampras and Ben Crenshaw)

26. *Hard work pays off.* (anyone who's ever played any sport seriously)

27. *Keep centered.* (the careers of Mikan, Russell, Chamberlain, Thurmond, Walton, and Kareem)

28. *There's no such thing as a bad bounce.* (but don't tell that to Tony Kubek, Bill Buckner, or Jack Tatum)

29. *Simplify, simplify.* (Don Larsen's no-windup, Willie's basket catch, the '66 Packers' power sweep)

30. *Learn how to sacrifice, and eventually good things will happen.* (Phil Rizzuto's life in baseball)

Why We're Not Baboons!

The human brain consists of ten basic structures, each with unique responsibilities: *medulla* (breathing, heartbeat, waking, sleeping), *pons* (dreaming), *reticular formation* (brain's sentinel), *thalamus* (relay station for sensory information), *cerebellum* (bodily movements, posture, equilibrium), *hippocampus* (long-term storage of information), *amygdala* (aggression, feeding, drinking, sexual behavior), *hypothalamus* (internal equilibrium), *cerebral cortex* (higher cognitive and emotional functions). And, present only in the confirmed sports nut, the little-known *triviata minor*, a tiny compartment that stores information of no seemingly earthly value, like Ted Lepcio's lifetime slugging percentage, the NBA center born in Hilo, Hawaii, and the name of the guy who tripped Dickie Moegle.

Now just think about it. What, after all is said and done, really separates us human beings from every other beast on the planet? Yep: it's the ol' *triviata minor*!

I mean, if you got a bunch of even the most alert, intelligent, and highly-developed apes together—chimpanzees, orangutans, gorillas, baboons, mandrills, you name it—and asked them to perform all the above major functions of the brain, they'd be able to do every last one of them. Every last one, of course, except those for which the *triviata minor* is solely responsible. That's right, ask the chimp (or orangutan or gorilla or baboon or mandrill) to breathe or take a nap or dream or stand up straight or walk a straight line or remember or fight or eat or drink or copulate or weep like a baby, and chances are the cunning simian will get an A+ (and a great big banana) for its efforts.

But ask the same alert, intelligent, highly-developed creature to tell you what's Whitey Lockman's real first name or which great Phillies starting pitcher ended his career by chopping up his toe with a lawnmower or who pinch-ran for little Eddie Gaedel or what Don Mueller and Donn Clendenon had in common or what made Dale Mitchell famous or where Win Wilfong went to college or who the two greatest college basketball players to wear uniforms with short-sleeve shirts were or why the name "Newberry" is important or which NBA player had as a vowel only one "y" in his last name or what's Ron Sobie's real last name or who the shortest Heisman Trophy winner ever was or who the first black player to win it was or which great NFL receiver came from Pittsburgh, TX, or who caught Fran Tarkenton's first NFL touchdown pass or what the "CH" on the Montreal NHL jersey stands for or who made the "spaghetti" racquet famous or who the smallest world-class male tennis player ever was or who the only male member of the World Golf Hall of Fame never to win a major is or who Edson Arantes do Nascimento is, and I'll bet the ranch that all you'd get from the stunned primate would be one of those vacant, idiotic looks.

So, parents of the world, *listen up!* The next time you think your kids are wasting their time by staring dumbly at those baseball cards or gluing themselves to the TV during the NCAAs or studying the box scores at the breakfast table or memorizing the entire

Encyclopedia of Football or playing Sports Trivia on the internet, think again. Fact is, they're simply developing that specialized, unique, undervalued, unappreciated, and glorious section of their brain that just happens to separate them from every beast on the planet who doesn't walk upright.

Emerson Transistor

As our planet hurtles madly toward the twenty-first century, we humans are perfectly content to fritter away much of our time playing with (and taking for granted) our hi-tech, megabitted, megahurted, microchipped, mini-sized, internetted, bewebbèd, compact-discèd toys. Nothing seems to boggle the mind these days, as we're inundated (daily it seems) with awesome technology that is smaller, faster, and more powerful and that allows us to communicate and interact with incrementally increasing ease and flexibility.

But: in the olden days of black-and-white Dumont TVs, klunky Philco radios, boxy Amana refrigerators, pop-up G.E. toasters, manual juice squeezers, hunt-and-peck typewriters, reel-to-reel tape recorders, Victrolas, and LPs, technological "oddities" and breakthroughs were indeed relatively few and far between. In fact, the first (and possibly only one) that occurred during my formative years and that comes to mind many decades later is the wondrous transistor radio.

How cute and adorable this little technological treasure seemed then! What a change of pace from the heavy, klunky, boxy, unwieldy, hardly portable behemoths we called radios: you know, those babies with the huge dials on either side, the vertical needle to indicate the stations, the big numbers (for those of us who were reading-impaired), and the long cords.

Anyway, it was around '54 or '55, I think, when they went into production and when my parents had the foresight to buy me one. Unbeknownst to them (and quite ironically), it was to become the ultimate instrument of deception, the ultimate symbol of filial revolt against parental constriction ever devised by humankind.

It was an Emerson: black, with the gold name "Emerson" emblazoned on its front. The thing was incredibly tiny (for '54 or '55, that is): I'd say about 4" high × 3" wide × 1" deep. It had tiny slats (good for collecting lint) all along its front, from which sound emanated; and a round dial that was microscopic for its time. All you had to do was turn it a speck—literally—and, as if magically, the station would change from Cousin Brucie to Alan Freed to Murray the K to a Knicks game. All on AM, of course! (You could only get FM on big radios, and *that* was for the express purpose of classical music and similar material for "adult" listening pleasure.) And most of the stations (especially the *important* ones like WINS and WMGM) came in pretty clearly.

All of this was way cool, to be sure, but there was one feature above all others that actually defined the essence of this new toy. To wit: it was so beautifully tiny that not only could you tote it around wherever you wanted, but best of all, you could hide it under the pillow after your bedtime curfew and listen to your heart's delight (even into the wee hours, or whenever the Knicks game ended). And all the while, your parents were blissfully unaware of your transgression, deception, and treachery!

(Parenthetically, I do remember that coincidentally, I had just discovered the wonders of Dostoevsky, having been given, a few weeks before the radio arrived, a Modern Library copy of *Crime and Punishment*. I can recall my curling up in the fetal position, turning the radio on, placing it furtively under the pillow, and pretending to be a modern-day Raskolnikov committing the perfect crime, only meters away from my oblivious parental "victims." I could further identify with the hero, since our Christian names—Robert, Rodion—began with the same two letters, and our Russian names— my father, né Grabelsky, had ancestors who came to this country from Odessa in the Ukraine—were, well, Russian.)

O, the sweet, sneaky, solitary sessions of sin stolen between Ipana and slumber! Like ol' Raskolnikov, I was pretty fastidious about my crime. First, I spent minutes getting the station just so. Then, I performed the adjustment of the volume with the digital dexterity of a safe cracker. Had to turn up the volume so I could hear through the pillow-foam, but not too loud: could get caught. There we go: *just right!* And there I lay, stiff as a board and cool as a cucumber, my ear pressed hard against my pillow to catch every delicious syllable; then, as I zeroed in on the Knicks game, I was mesmerized into a state of ecstasy by the mellifluent voice of one of my favorite announcers of all time, the great Marty Glickman.

Marty had a wonderful way of articulating, a sort of old-fashioned but clipped diction. He was also a talented creator of word-pictures, so that you could actually imagine the action, as if it were taking place right there under your pillow. And he got you really excited when a basket was scored, especially by one of the Knicks.

I remember that there were many more games broadcast on radio than shown on TV in those days (radio being the older of the two media, and much more advanced). In any case, I'm still grateful today that I got to listen to the performance of so many of the great old NBA players (most of them white, by the way: before Russ and Wilt came into the league, there were just a handful of African-Americans, including two Knicks: Ray Felix, from L.I.U. via the old

Baltimore Bullets; and my personal favorite, Nat "Sweetwater" Clifton, who came to the NBA by way of the Harlem Globetrotters). And it was through Glickman's verbal poetry that I got to enjoy the efforts of players like Neil Johnston, Paul Arizin, and Tom Gola (Philadelphia), Bob Cousy, Bill Sharman, and "Easy Ed" Macauley (Boston), Bob Pettit, Cliff Hagan, and Frank Selvy (St. Louis), Bob Davies, Bobby Wanzer, and Jack Twyman (Rochester), Dolph Schayes, Paul Seymour, and Johnny Kerr (Syracuse), Larry Foust, George Yardley, and Andy Phillip (Fort Wayne), George Mikan, Clyde Lovellette, and Slater Martin (Minneapolis); and, of course, all those great old Knicks: Vince Boryla, Clifton and Felix, Dick and Al McGuire, Harry Gallatin, Carl Braun, Ernie Vandeweghe (Kiki's Dad), Jim Baechtold. . . .

The game was, of course, a lot slower then (although probably just as physical as it is nowadays), but there were far fewer pyrotechnics than with today's version of roundball. Rather than watching huge physical specimens fly through the air and slam-dunk at will, or unbelievable athletes hit jumpers from deep in the corners with jeweler-like precision, you witnessed a slower, more strategic action develop, with dogged "weaves," two-handed bounce passes, backdoor plays. (Princeton's teams are traditionally a throwback to these kinds of "fundamentals.") Shots were also less violent: instead of dunks and jams, there were mostly lay-ups (including underhanded "scoops") and a variety of "set shots": two-handed sets (perfected by players like Schayes), one-hand pushes (Sharman was probably the best at it), and over-the-head "pop shots" (Braun's was my favorite). And Glickman's clipped, lilting voice was perfect for this ebb-and-flow type of action. Listening to him describe the action was like being lullabied to sleep (and I mean this only in the best sense!). On the other hand, his passion and excitement fanned your "Knicks fires," and you ended up biting your pillow in suspense more often than not. The contests were often low-scoring (in the sixties, seven-

ties, and eighties), particularly before the 24-second rule was instituted. But always exciting and, if you were a Knicks fan, frequently disappointing.

My most vivid memories are the games between the Knicks and
the Syracuse Nationals that Glickman used to call. They almost
always went down to the wire, with the Knicks losing by a point or
two in the dying seconds. And almost always, it was the dreaded
Dolph Schayes (ironically, an N.Y.U. grad) who did us in, always in
the same manner. It was always a see-saw affair, with Schayes being
virtually unstoppable and the Knicks making up for his offensive firepower with a balanced attack led by Braun, McGuire, and Gallatin.
"Sweets" always hit a key hook shot (off the glass, of course), and
Gallatin truly lived up to his name as a "horse" on the boards. But it
was always tied, 76–76, with about a minute to go.

*Knicks take it across the midcourt line. Now it's Caaaaaarl Braun pass-
ing it to McGuire. Tricky Dick has been dishing out the assists all game long,
so we can expect some more trickery from him in this, the closing minute.
McGuire dribbles, feints, gives it back to Braun. Here's Caaaaaarl at the top
of the key. He steps back for a two-hand pop from twenty-five feet: it's
gooooooooooooooooooooooood, like Nedick's! And the Nats call a time out
with but a mere ten seconds remaining and the Knicks ahead by a single
bucket, 78–76!*

I am swimming in a pool of sweat, my ear pressed even more
tightly than before to the pillow, my entire being tortured between,
on the one hand, the urge to scream out a series of ecstatic yelps at
the top of my lungs and with all my young might, and on the other,
the instinct to stifle my enthusiasm for fear of being caught in my
transgression and with my hand in the proverbial cookie jar. Now the
teams are back for the final, excruciating seconds.

*All right, fans, hold onto your hats! The Nats take it in. It's Paul
Seymour in-bounding it to Red Rocha, now back to Seymour. He dribbles,
shovels a pass to Schayes—it's almost stolen by Tricky Dick!—but no,*

Schayes holds on to the ball with three seconds left, he slices to his left, he drives past Gallatin, he lays it up, the buzzer sounds . . . it's good, and he's fouled! All right, it's seventy-eight to seventy-eight. Schayes steps up to the charity stripe with one foul shot to win it for Syracuse. He bounces the ball once, twice, three times. He lets it go . . . it's gooooooood, and the Nats win it in a squeaker!

Like a sickening, recurring nightmare, it is always the same scenario. Down to the final seconds. Knicks forge ahead. Then, with three seconds left, Schayes beats them at the buzzer with a three-point play. And as usual, I can't control myself: *shiiiiiiiiiiiiiiiiiiiit!*

I lie there, beside myself, not only miserable about the outcome, but now waiting for my father to gallop in, turn on the light, discover my Covert Operations, and confiscate the cursèd transistor for life! For three minutes, I lie there stock-still, expecting the worst. But I luck out, and once again Morpheus has guilefully inserted himself between me and catastrophe. In retrospect, I think the excitement of the deception, the novelty of hearing the games emanating from beneath my pillow out of this funny little black box, and the waiting in the dark for the worst to occur when the game was over all made listening to these sporting events among the most thrilling of all my experiences as a fan.

I'm not sure what happened to my little black Emerson transistor radio. I do remember several years later, in '58 (just after my beloved New York baseball Giants had moved to San Francisco), I still had it, because I used to listen to Les Keiter's re-enactments of the "new" Giants' games. At that point, it had seen better days: by now, its "face" was battered and cracked and crumbling, held together with numerous bits and pieces of variously colored freezer tape. Anyway, Keiter would read his "delayed" scripts to the clatter of ticker-tape and a steady stream of canned crowd roars in the background, all to make it seem authentic. Whenever a batter made contact (seconds earlier, at the "real" game), Les would simulate the *tock!* of bat against ball by using a sound effect created by hitting a block of wood with a stick. Despite the phoniness, and the decreased capability of 'ol Emmo to transmit anything resembling clarity, the games were still fun to listen to, especially for a Giants fan whose team had been cruelly ripped from its womb and transplanted in some faraway place where people acted weird and spoke with no discernible accent. (Ironically, I would move to that very place some thirty-five years later.) I remember one game in particular in which my Jints were trailing the Pirates, 8–0, going into the bottom of the ninth, when suddenly Mays, McCovey, & Co. went berserk and we rallied to win, 9–8.

So what happened to trusty ol' Emmo? As with the ultimate fate of my old baseball mitts and other assorted sports paraphernalia, I may never know. So what's the big deal? After all, wasn't it merely a hunk of black plastic with a jumble of rudimentary wires inside? Or was it more? Being at heart a hopeless Romantic by nature, I prefer to remember this beloved appliance as nothing less than a beautiful harbinger, a precursor to the revolution that so deeply marked the sixties.

Yes, in a decade distinguished by a noticeable absence of world wars or cataclysmic domestic conflict, by Eisenhower's eventless regime, Uncle Miltie, the nuclear family (and the twin concepts of obedience and "family values"), Levittown, diners, LPs, and friendly milkmen and gas station attendants, my little black Emerson transistor radio stands out in my mind as the lone bastion of rebellion and trickery, the sole symbol of pulling the wool over the watchful eyes of my parents. More than a mere emittor of sound waves, it did nothing less than prepare me for the violent, meteoric, unpredictable decade to come, allow me to begin to spread my adolescent wings and to subscribe regularly to a practice that is as natural as mother's milk to a nascent teen-ager: *rebellion!* Years before the onslaught, before casual drinking and heavier drinking and recreational grass and pre-marital sex and heavy rock and Sproul Hall at Berkeley and the Alma Mater statue at Columbia and the endless protests and the joke that was the draft, there was my Emerson transistor suckling me with its rebel's milk! Certainly, it fueled the fires of my sporting obsession, and for that, I am eternally grateful. But more than that, it allowed me to hone and develop the very weapons that would, later in life, contribute to my survival in an increasingly cruel world and to my continual battle against the Established Powers That Be: treachery, deviousness, deceit, foul play, covertness, insolence, disrespect, mischievousness.

Thanks, ol' Emmo, wherever your tired remains may be resting.

Acknowledgments

To paraphrase Yogi, I'd like to thank everyone who made these stories necessary.

My thanks to Richard Grossinger for his judicious editing; to Nancy Koerner for her creativity and tasteful design; to Emily Weinert for her compassionate shepherding; to Stephen Mitchell for his helpful suggestions and brotherly support; and to Rolf Olness for the generous loan of his classic baseball cards that appear on the cover of this book (I would've used *mine*, but . . .).

I am very grateful to a number of people who have enriched the considerable part of me that is athlete and sports fan: Ernie Fleishman, Bob Bell, Ralph Dupee, and Clarence Chaffee (my coaches); Sal Maglie, Jackie Robinson, Willie Mays, Ken Rosewall, Tony Trabert, Ben Hogan, Babe Didrickson, Jim Brown, John Unitas, Dolph Schayes, and Bob Cousy (the athletes I most admired growing up); Jim Gertz, Ray Rizzuti, Jim Blumstein, and Steve Weinstock (high-school friends who pushed me to excel); Al Gorfin, Jon Maksik, Bob Liss, and Nat Greenfield (camp friends who pushed me to excel); Fred Thaler, David deVries, and Gert and Phil Cabaud (good friends with whom I've shared a passion for sports); David Frantz, Alan Zahn, Mark Garrison, Mike Appelbaum, Joel Drucker, and Ron Goldberg (the best tennis buddies a guy could ask for); and Nat Mitchell, Ken Horn, Ted Bass, and Kris Moe (the best golf buddies a guy could ask for).

A special thanks to George Smith for keeping my heart beating, literally. And to the following people for keeping my heart beating, figuratively, with their unflagging friendship and support: Diane, Nicole, and Simone Cabaud, Lance and Mary Donaldson-Evans, Bill and Beth Jaquith, David and Joanne Frantz, Leo and Margaret Schwartz, Hank and Elayne Gardstein, Ken and Paula Horn, Seymon Ostilly, Hugh Herbert-Burns, Kathy McMahon, David Langley, Ron Tobin, Suzanne Fleischman, Rony and Rachel Herz, Valerie Light, Bill Reilly, and Gary Vogensen.

Finally, my deepest gratitude to a loving and giving family: Noah, Jennifer, and Sarah Mitchell; Nat and Irma Mitchell; Stephen Mitchell and Vicki Chang; Morris and Esther Biederman; Phyllis, Bruce, and Mara Clurman; Bob and Rose Abrams; Si and Lorraine Grabel; and, in memory, Perk and Judy Abrams; Moe and Elsie Clurman; Stan Clurman; Harold Clurman; and Joe and Ceil Grabelsky.

About the Author

Bob Mitchell was born in Brooklyn in 1944 and studied at Williams, Columbia, and Harvard, where he received a Ph.D. in French and Comparative Literature. He was a French professor for eleven years at Harvard, Purdue, and Ohio State, during which time he published four books on nineteenth- and twentieth-century French poetry. He entered advertising in 1981 as a copywriter, became a creative director at a number of New York agencies, and spent 1994 in Tel Aviv as a special consultant on commercial film writing and production. Since then, he has been spending his time writing books about his first love—sports.

Passionate about sports, as both spectator and participant, he has followed all major and minor sports since 1951, lettered in three sports at Williams College (soccer, squash, tennis), and has taught tennis professionally. He lives in Sonoma, California with his dog, Maglie.